UNSAFE ON ANY BURNER:
Misadventures of
a Rookie Cook

Bob —

Best Wishes

to Wisconsins Best

Cook!

UNSAFE ON ANY BURNER:

Misadventures of a Rookie Cook

FRED GOSMAN

BASHFORD & O'NEILL

MILWAUKEE

1998

Publisher's Cataloging-in-Publication
(*Provided by Quality Books, Inc.*)

Gosman, Fred G.
    Unsafe on any burner : misadventures of a rookie cook /
Fred Gosman. -- 1st ed.
    p. cm.
    Preassigned LCCN: 98-72947
    ISBN: 0-9627419-7-3

    1. Cookery. 2. Cookery--Humor. 3. Gosman, Fred G.
I. Title.
    TX714.G67 1998   641.5'0207
                                        QBI98-906

Manufactured in the United States of America
98765432
First Edition

Contents

Cody - when you read - try not to look at Jessica LOL

A Cook (?) Is Born!

I had an old-fashioned marriage. My wife cooked, and I ate.

At the time this seemed to make some sense. I performed all the household maintenance, like mowing the lawn, clearing the snow, and raking the leaves. Inside our home we jointly raised our two wonderful sons, Bob and Mike, now twenty-three and nineteen. Although my wife had many responsibilities, she never worked outside the home. We accepted our division of labor, and never spent a moment arguing about it.

Sadly, our unity in other aspects of our marriage wasn't as complete, and after twenty-two years together we divorced. All at once I was on my own, forced to cook. I was a true fish out of water: a Grey

FRED GOSMAN

without Poupon, a Chase without Sanborn, a Doughboy without Pillsbury. Suddenly I wished I had diced more and shovelled less.

The most basic of food questions perplexed me. Is it permissible to eat a morning bun in the evening? How does a shopper know if a can of evaporated milk is full?

I initially tried to skip meals, in order to minimize my cooking needs. This strategy lasted until my third hunger pain. Next, I dropped in on friends at dinnertime. Most were understanding for a while, but I needed to change my game plan when two of them sent me moving cards with no addresses.

Thank goodness for my neighbor, Mary. She took pity on me, and opened up her home four or five times. But soon I sensed she resented my presence: "You here again?" she'd ask, eyes looking heavenward. "I promise to go grocery shopping tomorrow," I'd respond, repeating my normal refrain. Sensing her anger, I resorted to flattery. "Mary, you look lovely this evening," I said. But she wasn't charmed. "Free food improves eyesight," she shot back. Eventually she took away my dining card, and urged me to try making complex, sophisticated entrees, like jello.

As I was sure this was way beyond me, I was now forced to dine in restaurants. I saw so much of the Colonel I considered enlisting. Manny's Gyros had eighteen different sandwiches, and I was familiar with every one. Things got so bad, I once attempted to supersize my petit filet in a fine French restaurant. After two months of eating out, I was ready for change, since that was all that remained in my bank account.

But the brave new world of cooking was foreign to me! A penne used to be a loafer, and a shallot was a movie reviewer. Samosa was a dictator, and Al Dente a third baseman on the old Brooklyn Dodgers. A pinot noir was one of those fancy things women wear to bed on special nights.

As a rookie chef I had so much to do! Buy housewares. Shop for groceries. Organize my pantry. Prepare edible food. Learn to be a good host. And each was a mystery to me.

Of course, I could begin by relying on the little cooking experience I already had. Unfortunately, in college I usually ate prepared frozen foods. Almost every meal was a Banquet, or a Swanson, depending upon which one was on special at my local market. To this day, even when a gourmet meal is placed in front of me, my thumb and index finger touch, a reflex born of years of peeling off foil meal covers.

During my marriage I did cook periodically. Generally you would find me at the barbecue, but even there competence eluded me. Once I ruined the season-ending party for Bob's soccer team by putting an entire bag of charcoal in the grill; the fire was so hot, all the hot dogs burned. More typically, I struggled to merely keep the fire aglow, and felt blessed if I still had lighter fluid remaining when dinner was served.

Occasionally I dabbled in the kitchen itself. I would prepare bowls of Special K or Wheaties for Bob and Mike. This was a no-brainer: I was certainly no cereal killer. I would also make sandwiches for myself and the boys. And I'd usually help wash the dishes two to three times a week.

Briefly, in about the fifth year of my marriage, I did flirt with the cooking life. But it wasn't a confidence-building experience. One time I attempted to remove a casserole dish from the oven with only one potholder. The hot dish began to slip as I lifted it toward the counter. Instinctively my free hand grabbed hold to prevent the dish from falling. Ouch! I suffered a mild burn. As did my wife, when she saw that our vinyl kitchen floor was permanently marred where the hot dish had landed.

Despite this history of kitchen ineptitude, a miracle occurred as I confronted the realities of my new life: I began to love to cook. I actually became quite comfortable in the kitchen, and learned how to use new appliances and gadgets. I developed a

UNSAFE ON ANY BURNER

love of spices, and experimented with new cuisines. I mastered many delicious, simple recipes. I enrolled in cooking classes, and actually became a relaxed, competent host. And my social life soon revolved around food (and really began to cook).

A second miracle happened, too: I lost fifty (50!) pounds. I had been overweight for thirty years, but in the process of my culinary transformation I actually developed new eating habits that, thus far, have remained with me for five years. In this book I describe what they are, and have included some simple, healthy recipes that have helped me stay on track.

Along the way, extraordinary things occurred. I destroyed a blender and a towel rack. Almost got into a fight with a supermarket employee. Found my fondue fork at the local bank. Watered some artificial flowers. Claimed spaghetti sauce stains on my ceiling were a stencil. Learned there's nothing like making meatloaf to get your hands really clean. Served Minute Rice to Asians. Locked myself out of my apartment ten minutes before a dinner party. Ran the first personal ad in history seeking dates with women who cook. Prepared a gourmet dinner for a major food critic.

UNSAFE ON ANY BURNER details these events, and is the record of my stumbling, bumbling journey toward kitchen competence and weight loss.

FRED GOSMAN

It's a story of perseverance against great initial frustration. It's a story of healthy change in a time of crisis. It's a story of people needing people.

But on its most basic level it's a story of hope, and clearly demonstrates the growth a man is capable of simply because he's hungry.

Gearing
Up

Houseware Horrors

I initially took the coward's path in order to avoid confronting the unknown world of housewares: I ate out.

The key to this sophisticated strategy was Manny's Gyros, a neighborhood institution half a block from my apartment. I'd stop there most nights after work, picking up a big deli sandwich and a piece of mediocre cheesecake. This routine varied only on Tuesday evenings, when the freshly made cheesecake actually tasted good.

Sad to say, Manny's took its toll. I could put up with the monotony. I could put up with the expense. I could even put up with the smells. But I could not live without sleep, and Manny's heartburn was killing me.

I considered eating healthier fare in other restaurants, but Manny's prices were the lowest around. I bought some Total and milk, and ate that for a week. But when my friend Mary informed me I wasn't giving my body enough variety, I ceased the habit. So I made a life-changing decision: I would learn to cook.

Ever mindful of my budget, I initially relied upon my friends to meet my housewares needs. Mary lent me a small frying pan. Roger and Linda let me use some old juice glasses and three chipped dinner plates. For silverware I reused the plastic utensils Manny put in my nightly take out.

Unfortunately, my presentation skills didn't impress Mary when I invited her over for hamburgers. I'm not sure what set her off, but probably seeing Manny's name on the napkins and straws was no plus. "You set the worst table in the Western Hemisphere," she said. "If you don't go housewares hunting with me on Saturday, I'll never lend you another thing."

Talk about pressure. Mary was a convenient source for lots of essential cookery. I couldn't let her cut me off, so the following Saturday we cut out for the mall.

Sad to say, in mi casa, no Mikasa. As a newly separated man, my finances were in turmoil. Dishes had to be low end, so I selected basic earthenware, rather than china. I found a set on clearance consisting of a dinner plate, and salad plate, and bowl. Each was plain white, with a blue ring around the outside. A set cost just four bucks apiece. With Mary's go ahead, I bought eight sets, and they've served me well.

Money was an issue in selecting pots, too. I explained my budget realities to Julia, my department store salesperson, but she didn't immediately get the price point. "Of course you'll want your pots to be ONS," she declared. "Pardon me," I said. "You know, the ONS," Julia explained. "Calphalon, Anolon, Circulon. You deserve the best."

I looked at the price tags of the ONS and practically fell over. These were far out of my range. "Julia," I said, "many of your shoppers love ONS, more power to them. But my budget is limited. The only ON I can afford is Teflon. I'm afraid I'm more into OFF, as in off-price."

I eventually selected a five piece T-Fal set for about sixty dollars. I could have saved twenty bucks by selecting a lighter and flimsier set, but Mary talked me out of it, and I'm glad she did. Cooks use their pots all the time, for many years. If they are heavier, and have a more permanent feel, your cooking experience will be far more pleasurable. So if you can, spend the extra money on cookware you'll enjoy.

Assembling my wonderful T-Fal pots when we returned home was not without tension, however. I could not figure out how to put on the contraptions on top, the ones that allow you to control whether the steam vents or not. "Do you want me to do it?" Mary asked. "No," I responded. "Piece of cake."

First, a little background. The only course I've ever flunked in my life is eighth grade shop. And I hadn't a clue what to do with my T-Fal. I kept trying to affix the darn things, but success eluded me. Each time I thought they were permanently attached to the lids, they'd mockingly disengage. I was ready to reach for the Crazy Glue.

I was getting angrier and angrier. This was ridiculous; the pots were supposed to do the venting, not me! After bemusedly observing my discomfort for fifteen minutes, Mary bartered her skills for a glass of wine and put the gizmos on in seconds, only twice saying, "Piece of cake, huh?"

With dishes and now pots out of the way, I still needed flatware. That next day I went shopping alone, as Mary had a class. As you might guess, basic stainless steel was plenty good enough for me. I did, though, resist the sets that were outrageously light or flimsy to the touch. I bought a service for eight for about forty dollars, and they have been exactly what I needed.

UNSAFE ON ANY BURNER

I decided I'd like a mixer, and bought a little hand one, for about fourteen dollars. I wanted to see if I could make a better cheesecake than Manny. A mixer is a really nice thing to have, for whipping flour with eggs, or whipping cream cheese or regular cream. I was intimidated by it at first—couldn't figure out how to insert the beaters. But then I noticed the little notches one inch from the end of each beater, and when I aligned them properly with the appropriate openings in the main unit, I was in business.

Since I love mashed potatoes, I bought a good peeler, and would urge you to do so, too. Not the old-fashioned kind, for a buck or two, but the ergonomically friendly swivel variety, for four to six dollars. These almost make peeling fun. And I knew I'd have to open cans of beans and soup, so I bought a nice manual can opener. Here, too, avoid the cheapo models. Buy the oversized ones, for five or six bucks. They lock on to the can, and make turning far easier.

Be selective buying measuring spoons and cups, as well. I had a real adventure in one store. The sales clerk was attempting to interest me in a set of stainless steel measuring cups, for twenty-five dollars. But after examining them, I had concerns. "I can't read the size of the cup," I said. "It looks like it's written in Greek." "But these are specially contoured for your hand," the clerk replied. "And I'm grateful for that," I added. "But how will I know if I'm measuring a third or a half of a cup?" "These will last forever," the clerk proudly boasted. "And don't worry," she added. "The size of the measuring cup is also written on the bottom." Even I knew this was no advantage. I could visualize myself turning a full cup of flour upside down to find out exactly how much I was spilling!

So I bought a much less expensive plastic set. But even on these the sizes are often difficult to read. So, only buy measuring spoons and cups with BIG, BOLD, EASY-TO-READ type.

I did splurge on something totally frivolous. I was browsing in the housewares department of a local department store and came upon a tea kettle with Bugs Bunny on it. The handle was in the shape of a carrot, and the spout looked like Daffy Duck. I've always loved Bugs, and the kettle really tickled me, so I spent the twenty-nine bucks. For a smile a day, I still consider it cheap.

Rummage sales were a great source of useful items I might not have otherwise purchased. One day I saw a new wok on sale, in its original box, for just three dollars. "I'll get it," I said. "Mary will be shocked to see that I own a specialty appliance."

She did just about fall over when she entered my apartment and saw me proudly working my wok.

"Who'd you borrow the wok from?" she asked. I ignored the insult. I felt so proud, so much like an insider.

Armed with this success I became overconfident, and started a housewares run when I should still have been walking. I came upon a crepe maker at a rummage sale and I pounced. "Another specialty appliance," I said. "Whoopie!"

To this day it lies unused. I haven't yet figured it out. Once I tried to lift off what I thought was the top, sort of a dome-like thing, to see where the batter would go. But I received a major surprise. It didn't lift off. Apparently, it is the top; the batter somehow rests right there. One of these days I'll get up the courage to confront it again. But at least I learned a lesson, and now make sure I know how something works before I buy it.

I quickly discovered that stocking a kitchen is always a work in progress. I learned I needed a pastry brush from a recipe that said "brush on olive oil." I discovered the need for a thermometer when reading about the health hazards of serving undercooked Thanksgiving turkey. I bought a trivet after scalding my table. And my friend Harriet's laughter at seeing me attempt to empty a mixing bowl without a rubber spatula drove me to buy one.

The biggest rookie mistake I made was buying

things piecemeal. Like knives. I initially bought a paring knife for cutting vegetables. Then I bought a bigger knife for cutting meat, and a giant one for cutting squash in half. I would have been better off buying a complete set. Not only would I have saved money, but all the handles would match, and I would have received the wooden block that keeps the knives safely stored when not in use.

Same with Tupperware. I initially bought it one piece at a time. No one item was expensive, but the dollars added up. Eventually, as I discovered I loved to cook and needed ever more containers, I bit the bullet and bought the large box with enough pieces for two lifetimes.

I did resist a few gadgets and gimmicks. The mayonnaise knife was a total nonstarter. In fact, I thought it was a joke. It's a special knife, a little like a rubber spatula, that allows you to get out every last drop from your mayonnaise jar. Is this a large problem in our society?

Nor was I tempted by serving bowls that told you what was in them. Don't guests realize they're eating "PASTA" or "POPCORN" by the time the bowl is empty? And I felt the same about other cutesy messages. At a friend's house I once was greeted with a "YOU DID IT!" when I finished a bowl of potato chips. And a pasta bowl once gave me a "THAT'A BOY!" Maybe it's a self-esteem issue, but

UNSAFE ON ANY BURNER

I'm not totally comfortable receiving praise and encouragement from serving dishes.

Despite all my purchases, I still covet a few gadgets, and might purchase them in the future. A long fork with special tines, for use in snaring pickles from pickle jars, seemed to make sense. It certainly beats fingers, although I own some chopsticks, and these might be fun utensils for this purpose. And I've promised myself a vacuum wine saver, and will buy it if I ever have any leftover wine.

Of course, it's one thing to own a gadget, and quite another to find it. I just automatically throw my gadgets in a special drawer. We all have one of these: it's the one that, ten gadgets ago, we said can't hold another gadget. Because it's so stuffed, the minutes spent hunting for a gadget often exceed the minutes saved by utilizing the gadget.

Even if you eventually find what you're looking for, you still need to put back all the other gadgets you took out during your search. And inevitably you're rushed when you do this, and force the items in as quickly as you can. As a result, the next time you open the drawer to start your gadget search, it's stuck. And in forcing the issue, something always breaks.

Small breakage, however, can be tolerated. Destruction of a new appliance is entirely another matter. During my post-wok euphoria, I bought a basic blender, with ten speeds, for about twenty-five dollars. But the first time I used it, I broke it. I was trying to make an easy cheesecake recipe, a cheesecake pie. I thought it seemed reminiscent of Manny's. I was to blend cream cheese with whole milk, do some other stuff, and then pour the mixture into a graham cracker crust. Well, the recipe said to blend till smooth.

Unfortunately, it never said that the cream cheese had to be softened. So I married up my rock-hard cream cheese with the milk, and put my blender in overdrive. Of course, nothing happened; the cream cheese was too hard. But I didn't recognize this as the problem. It was the first time I had ever used a blender, and I assumed I was doing something wrong. In frustration, I kept turning the blender on, hoping this time that the blend would take. Suddenly there was a funny smell coming from the unit, the odor of a burned-out engine. Upset with myself, I took the blender and threw it in the garbage. NOT my finest hour as a fledgling chef.

Then there was the destruction of the towel rack. A dinner guest bought me a large, wooden paper towel rack. It was a wonderful gift, but when hanging it on the wall, I didn't have the correct screws, so I made do with two small nails. Unfortunately, the rack lay unsteady against the wall. So I took out a really large nail and tried to hammer it into the middle of the unit.

Barbara advised me not to do it. "Those nails are too big," she said. "You'll split the towel rack in two." "Don't be silly," I said. "The towel rack is made of a thick piece of wood." My initial piercing of the wood was successful. "See, I told you," I said. "You had nothing to worry about." To prove the point, I raised the hammer high and delivered a forceful downward stroke. Unfortunately, the towel rack also had a stroke, and split in two. Barbara tried to be a sport, and said she forgave me. But when she left that evening, she was humming "If I Had a Hammer."

In addition to a towel rack, I still lack many things: lemon reamer, pastry wheel, banana tree, tortilla warmer, salsa server, paella dish, ice bucket, tea steeper, terra cotta serveware, yeast and candy thermometer, pizzelle baker, gravy skimmer, asparagus steamer, ice cream maker, fryer, pasta maker, juicer, battery-powered grater, rolling pin cover, potato baking rods, cookbook holder, salad spinner, strawberry huller, corn holders, fish knife, lattice pastry roller, clam knife or mallet, icing comb, microwave egg poacher, turnover press, bundt pan, pancake rings, apple wedger, ravioli cutter, canelle knife, pastry blender, cherry pitter, tart rings, fish lifter, fruit press, oyster shucker, meat mincer, caviar cooler, turkey lifter, waffle maker, spaghetti measure, and corrugated wedger.

And I'd like some of these items. Can I confess something? I'm jealous of new brides. They usually have a kitchen shower, and receive lots of great items free. I'm tired of spending money. Newly divorced guys deserve showers, as do women who as yet have not married.

Friends who read this book, are you paying attention? I want a shower. It doesn't need to be an elaborate affair. Invitations can be by phone. A house party is fine. If necessary, I'll even do the cooking. What a great chance for us to converse, and discover what's new in each others' lives.

And oh yes, one other thing. Out of consideration for your busy schedules, gifts (see list above) needn't be wrapped!

FREDDY'S TOP EIGHT
KITCHEN STOCKING POINTS

- When selecting cookware, don't settle for pot luck.

- Drawer searches usually take twice as long as you think they will.

- Real men don't use jar openers.

- The color of an item is unimportant if it is stored in a cabinet.

- Never underestimate the number of Tupperware containers manufacturers can fit in one box.

- The smaller the kitchen, the greater the number of gadgets in it.

- Don't use plastic spoons to stir a frying pan.

- Nobody has ever used every blade that came with their food processor.

In Search of the Doughboy

Now that I was the proud owner of sundry pots and pans, I needed to purchase groceries. But this was a new experience for me, and I approached it with trepidation. I quickly discovered there was a lot going on at my friendly, local market, and that people were often the most interesting things on display.

On my initial trips to the supermarket, I was totally dumbfounded by the variety of products I discovered. Cheerios has gone frosted, Wheaties now has raisins. There are seemingly forty-six different kinds of vinegar, and four hundred sixteen varieties of Hamburger Helper.

Historical figures and even modern celebrities all fight it out for market share. Robin Hood Flour;

UNSAFE ON ANY BURNER

Popeye Spinach; Newman's Own Salad Dressings. But often the names don't work. Take Joan of Arc Green Beans. Sort of a funny name for a vegetable brand, isn't it? Can anyone see Joan going "Ho! Ho! Ho!?"

Thousands and thousands of products catch the eye. Traditional, low fat, non fat, low sodium, calcium added, fiber enriched, organic, etc. It's not at all like the good old days, when Heinz had fifty-seven varieties and the biggest decision was shaved or sliced.

Although products are abundant in supermarkets, employees aren't. Most of those you ask for help respond, "Sorry, I'm a rep, I'm not with the store." Often the staff is totally unfamiliar with the inventory, especially the newer ethnic items.

Once I was in Indianapolis and wanted to buy some hummus at a good-sized food market. Hummus is really delicious. It's a paste made from chickpeas, and you can eat it as a dip or a spread. Since a friend had sent me there, and was sure they stocked it, my only responsibility was to find it.

I approached seven different employees and asked, "Where is the hummus?" Each and every one responded, "Where is the WHAT?" They assured me they didn't carry it. Finally, a woman in line referred me to a market three miles distant, where I bought it. When I eventually complained to my friend about her bum advice, she insisted that she was correct, and bet me five dollars that she could find it in the original market within twenty seconds of entry. It only took her eight.

I eat hummus all the time. Here's the recipe for Freddy's Black Bean Hummus. Eat it as a dip, or for lunch or dinner in a pita, and your tummy will be very happy. And it stays well in the refrigerator for a few days.

Here's what you do: Pour into a food processor two cans of drained and rinsed garbanzo beans and a can of drained and rinsed black beans. Add three tablespoons of olive oil, and five of lemon juice. Add lots of garlic, six to ten cloves, and a teaspoon of cumin. Process until you achieve the consistency you desire. This is low in fat, high in fiber, and tastes wonderful!

Hummus purists will immediately note the absence of tahini from my recipe. Tahini is sesame seed paste. For classic hummus, you might want to add it. I don't put it into mine because tahini has lots of fat.

Even if I'm lucky enough to eventually find the garbanzo beans/chickpeas, I have trouble locating other items. To lessen my frustration, I seek counsel from fellow shoppers. But this can prove dangerous. I once asked a lady if Diet Dr. Pepper was any good. She responded, "I don't drink it, but my husband does." And before I could restrain her, she set off on a search to find him. Unfortunately, the gentleman was in the motor oil aisle, and was difficult to locate. Cost me five minutes, and turned out he drank RC.

I once got so tired of receiving inaccurate, contradictory information from fellow shoppers that I blocked an entire aisle with my cart. Really. And I said, "No one passes until we reach consensus on the location of the sweetened condensed milk." Not exactly classy, but it worked! After consulting among themselves for ninety seconds, my hostages correctly informed me it could be found on aisle seven.

When I fantasize, I dream of stores that are alphabetical. You want bread, find the "B's." Hungry for tuna? Check out the "T's." Is this as crazy as it sounds?

Certain sections of the grocery store caused me special stress, and the deli counter usually brought out my wurst. One day a sign read, "BOGOF Turkey Breast, $5.99." I thought and thought. What was BOGOF? A new Rumanian supplier? A special, seasoned variety? So I asked, and got a simple answer. "Buy One, Get One Free."

I love "Take A Number" systems at deli counters, so customers know exactly when it will be their turn to be served. In fact, I won't buy a thing if there's a ton of people milling about and such a system isn't present. Number dispensers take all the tension out of waiting. You can eye new varieties of meats and salads rather than needing to keep your eyes focused on the suspicious-looking, late-arriving matron whose hand is poised to shoot skyward the instant the clerk says, "Next."

The canned vegetable aisle also caused me tension. I had extraordinary trouble finding garbanzo beans. As I indicated earlier, another name for them is chickpeas. So where do I look? In the "B's," for beans, or the "P's," for peas? And often the cans would be neither place, but instead could be found with the packaged beans, two aisles over, or in the Mexican section. It's time for the world to reach consensus on what to call these things.

The meat section continues to mystify me. Why is cubed steak not cubed? And when it comes to smoked ham, I'll never understand why people pay a premium for the butt. I've actually learned a little bit about fowl. Know that a roaster is older than a fryer, and that a capon is a "fixed" young rooster. And am astute enough to safely stand out of the way when six working moms enter a store at five-thirty in the afternoon and simultaneously race for the one remaining rotisserie chicken.

I often spend a few minutes on the gadget aisle, seeing if there is anything I need for my kitchen. I usually find I already own most of what's there, and feel a tad embarrassed. Plus, walking this section is not devoid of risk. As a six-footer, I inevitably bump my head on Rubbermaid pitchers dangling from the ceiling.

The freezer aisle is an adventure unto itself. Ninety per cent of it seems to be devoted to frozen pizza. I really don't spend much time in this section, as I buy few prepared items, although I have thought of a business opportunity. It is sometimes so incredibly COLD in this aisle, someone should rent out shawls, and charge by the minute.

As a rookie I was astonished by the number of items in the produce section. Ten kinds of lettuce, and new things like daikon and jicama. Quite a shock to someone expecting the carrots and cukes of his childhood.

Plus, some of the particulars of the produce section caused me initial concern. For starters the signage often seemed a little odd. The pineapple, for example, claimed to be "Jet Fresh." How else could it have come, by train?

And have you ever thought about how arbitrary it is that some fruits and vegetables are sold by the pound, and some by the piece? It's a little weird, isn't it? Take lettuce. Iceberg is only available by the head, but all other varieties are sold by the pound. Apples, peaches, plums, and bananas are sold by the pound, oranges and grapefruit by the piece. Bell peppers and green beans are sold by the pound, but cukes, mangoes, pineapples, kiwi, and avocados are sold by the piece.

It's also funny that some items can be bought only in bunches. Why can't I pick and choose as much parsley or dill or cilantro as I want, as with green beans or strawberries, and pay by the pound? And how come scallions can never be purchased by the piece?

Whether you buy produce by the pound, piece, or bunch, you will need to bag it. But the plastic bags provided are usually so difficult to open, it's amazing more of us don't get scurvy.

On my first shopping trips, I really struggled with these bags. Strangers needed to open them for me. Finally, someone advised me to wet my fingers and slide them along the edge. Presto! Even so, I often can't tell which is the end of the bag that opens. I would back legislation to require all grocery stores to adopt a standardized format, so that the bags would always tear off "top first" or "bottom first."

Occasionally, the "fruits" you meet in the produce section are fellow shoppers! Some people are incredibly picky about their apples, taking hours to find a delicious Delicious. I dubbed them "Apple Fondlers." For every apple they buy, they touch fifteen. If they ever committed a crime, the police would have to dust the entire produce section.

I usually put in my bag the first seven apples that I touch, and frankly have rarely had a bad apple. But I have had a little excitement. Once a very attractive woman was standing next to me at the apple bin, and made meaningful eye contact. It wasn't just a chance gaze, it was more like a long stare. I mentally kicked myself for putting off the beard trim, and pulled in my tummy to appear more trim.

But then, much to my disappointment, the true object of her affection became obvious. "Do you really want that third apple you put in your bag?" she asked. The lady was a Fondler. I'd have let her make me an offer, but we were in a suburban market crosstown, and I was unfamiliar with the nuances of local ordinances regarding apple scalping.

One also confronts the "Banana Gropers," shoppers who go bananas about their bananas. These people are texture challenged, spending hours searching for the quintessential perfect banana. Apparently for them the vast majority of bananas are either "too soft" or "too hard."

I've often fantasized about promoting a competition between the Apple Fondlers and the Banana Gropers. Maybe the World Wrestling Federation would be interested, if not the Produce Marketing Board. Apple cores and banana peels could be placed in a wrestling ring. The last shopper standing could receive first fondling/groping rights for an entire month.

As if shopping under these conditions isn't aggravating enough, one needs to also be on the lookout for children acting less than perfectly. When you come across a screamer, you say to the parent, "What a cute child," but what you really mean is "Sure glad he's not mine."

I witnessed two truly original parenting approaches to this common problem. One mom pulled a small sign out of her purse and calmly held it high. "Tantrum in Progress" it read. Took all the pressure off her, and the child regained control quickly.

The other mom was even more theatrical. She had a five-year-old girl. The little dear lay down right in the middle of the busiest aisle and started yelling, kicking, and screaming. Do you know what this mom did? She lay down right next to her child. Started yelling, and kicking, and screaming. Within three seconds her daughter stood up and said, "Mom, this is embarrassing. Let's go!"

FREDDY'S TOP EIGHT GROCERY POINTS

- The minute you become familiar with a store, the manager will announce a renovation.

- The Pillsbury Doughboy's sister is Poppie.

- Never touch more than fifty per cent of the apples in the bin.

- Most supermarket cart pushers should enroll in a crash course in safety.

- Picky produce shoppers should be required to buy fifty per cent of the items they touch.

- The two items you need most will always be at opposite ends of the store.

- Mr. Clean's first name, believe it or not, is Veritably.

- Never trust a seafood manager you can't smell.

The Express Lane
Is an Oxymoron

Finally, after all the crowded aisles and frustrating searches, you are prepared to check out. And that's where the nightmare really begins.

Finding the express lane in most modern supermarkets is rather easy. Just look for the line with twenty-three people in it. If I know that supermarkets need extra aisles open during busy periods, shouldn't management?

Anyway, I'm always nervous entering a self-proclaimed express lane, because I don't really know the technical definition of an "item." There I am, standing in an aisle that allows "ten items or less." I have in my cart five loose baking potatoes, four loose oranges, two loose lemons, and a carton of orange juice. How many items do I have, twelve or four?

But what if I decide I need more potatoes, and substitute a ten-pound bag of potatoes for the four loose ones? I would now have a large bag of potatoes, four loose oranges, two loose lemons, and a carton of orange juice. My item total would now be either four or eight, even though I have approximately sixteen more potatoes than previously. And if the lemons and oranges weren't loose, but were in bags, the situation gets even murkier.

Selecting a good checkout aisle is of course the true test of your ability as a shopper. I never leave this to chance. I take a long look at every cart in every line to see how full they are. I also size up the shoppers. Which look like credit card users, or check writers? Who fits the profile of the dreaded checker kibbitzer?

I never resort to line-jumping, since I had observed the futile antics of Line Jumping Larry during an early shopping trip. I was in the back of a long checkout line, and Larry was directly in front of me. Suddenly there was steady customer movement in the line two over. Larry instantly shot over there, only to discover that each of the remaining shoppers in his new line had exceptionally full carts. He gazed at me forlornly, his eyes silently inquiring, "Will you let me back in?" I smiled pleasantly back at him, my body language clearly communicating, "Don't even think of it."

While I slowly advanced toward the register, Larry kept jumping from line to line. Each move was counterproductive. Once the person four ahead of him triggered a lengthy price check. When he moved elsewhere, a lengthy coupon expiration date protest waylaid him. With each debacle, Larry's frustration grew more noticeable. Meanwhile, I was advancing to the register quite nicely.

After each setback, Larry would look my way, his eyes renewing his earlier plea for skips. I pretended I didn't notice. Suddenly I realized the stakes: Larry's ego was on the line, and he had a strong need to beat me to check out.

"Can't you open a new line?" he frantically shouted to the nearest checker, as he began to fully comprehend his competitive disadvantage. Larry started throwing items out of his cart onto the floor, to qualify for access to one of the express lanes, but suddenly one of the two express lines closed, and the remaining line was twice as long.

When I eventually checked out, Larry was still three back in the line two over, his face redder than the tomato soup I had seen in his cart. Incredibly, as I departed the store, he shot me an obscene gesture. But in truth I can't say I blame him. In retrospect, I probably shouldn't have waved goodbye!

Although I'm glad a new line wasn't opened for

Larry, it's nice when one occasionally does open. Unfortunately, this can cause chaos, even tempting "one-line" shoppers. The only thing a checker opening a new line should say is, "I can help the next in line here." Anything else is invitation to riot.

Seriously, what would Jesus Christ do if he was fourth in line and a checker opened the aisle two over? Would he allow the people ahead of him to enter that line first? Or would he pretend he didn't recognize the injustice and join the mad scramble for favored position like the rest of us?

I've developed a variety of methods to entertain myself while waiting in the checkout line. I play "cart psychologist," examining the contents of the carts of fellow shoppers trying to determine what makes them tick. If a lady with a mink coat is buying house brands, I figure she's experiencing tough times. If I see someone with lots of cheese and sausage, I mentally review the highlights of last fall's CPR class.

I also sing and hum to myself to pass the time, and it's not always appreciated. One day as I was in especially fine voice the lady in front of me said, "I could do without the concert." I was totally speechless. I didn't know what to say. Truthfully I wanted to hit her over the head with my zucchini, but it was out of season and expensive as heck. I stopped singing, but made a mental note to send her a CD if I ever record one. And two weeks later, a different shopper asked, "Don't you know any instrumentals?"

Finally, after a seemingly endless (but rarely uneventful) wait, I approach the register. Here I have a tip: Push your cart in BACKWARDS, or if you don't, PRECEED it. It is much easier to unload, since you don't have to reach over the higher section of the cart, where a child would sit, to reach the heavy items like laundry detergent and twelve-packs of soda. Unloading your cart this way might look funny, but your back will thank you.

Soon your entire financial well-being is in the hands of a faceless, high-tech scanner. I know we're all a tad suspicious of its accuracy, but I've only found two mistakes in four years of shopping. Each time I was overcharged a dime for pita bread, and received the item free when I informed management.

Lately, though, I've become a little paranoid about one aspect of my grocer's increasingly high-tech world. As a conscientious shopper, I scan my store card when I enter the store to receive bonus coupons. But the only ones I seem to receive are for products like deodorant and mouthwash. There's never any peanut butter, or ice cream, or good old salad dressing. Makes me wonder.

Unfortunately, this high-tech world isn't long on

trust. Once I ate an apple while I was shopping. I wasn't trying to shoplift, or anything like that. I was just hungry. I even kept the apple core in my cart, to remind me to inform the cashier of my snack. But when I told her, a nightmare began.

"What kind of apple did you eat?" she brusquely asked. "A Delicious," I responded. "How do I know that?" she asked, pointing out that apples vary in price and only Delicious were on sale. "Barring an x-ray, I guess you'll have to take my word for it," I responded.

"And what size was this alleged Delicious?" she asked. "Pardon me," I responded. "It's not an alleged Delicious. It's a Delicious." "Did you weigh it?" she asked. "No, I didn't," I confessed.

We were silent for a time, at a clear impasse. I seized the initiative, and facetiously asked, "Didn't Newton use a McIntosh to calculate a mathematical formula that determines an apple's weight once the size of its core is known?" Wrong question. The cashier called over the manager, who looked as if he was having a difficult day. He proceeded to actually form circles with his fingers, trying to have me acknowledge the approximate size (and therefore the likely weight) of my disputed appetizer.

Soon the people behind me in line started grousing about the delay. Not wanting to upset them further, I asked the manager to estimate the weight of the heaviest apple in the store. I multiplied times the cost per pound of the most expensive apple variety he carried, and gave my money to the cashier. Next time I'll snack elsewhere.

Even though I insist on paying for items I've eaten prior to checking out, I generally try to do everything I can to lower my tape total. Unfortunately, the loss-leader of the week often causes me intense aggravation. This is the item that's given away free or at minimal cost with a certain qualifying purchase. Despite hearing the explanations hundreds of times, I'm never sure if some of the sale items I have in my cart count toward the required total or not.

Often I buy packages of pasta, which won't spoil, to ensure that I spend enough. Or toilet paper. If I see it for sixty-nine cents for four rolls, I'm a buyer. But I live alone, and during a recent cleaning I discovered I was the proud owner of forty-four such packages. I'm now temporarily out of the toilet paper business, and have resolved to entertain more.

I also sometimes have trouble selecting the item that is the bargain. Once I returned home and discovered I had paid ninety-eight cents for a carton of eggs instead of the promotional price of thirty-four. Turns out I purchased large eggs. Only the extra large were available at the reduced price.

UNSAFE ON ANY BURNER

My milk crisis was even more frustrating. Talk about futility. This was probably the most embarrassing moment in all my grocery experience.

The house brand gallon of milk was but eighty-eight cents. By mistake I bought a national brand (what the heck, it too was white). At checkout I was charged $2.59. Frankly, I should have cut my losses, learned my lesson, and departed at once.

But I was not that smart. It became the ever-dangerous "matter of principle." I paid the checker, indignantly marched to the dairy cooler, and selected the house brand milk. Then I needed to enter the customer service line to make my appeal, and there were seven people ahead of me. Some were buying lottery tickets, some paying their phone bills, some presenting a coupon left at home the previous day. For fifteen minutes I stood in line, with fears of my blood pressure rising and my milk spoiling. Eventually I arrived at the front of the line, only to learn that I was ineligible for the special, as my tape total was too low!

More typically, however, my tape total is substantial. So I try to save money by using coupons whenever I can. But I don't seem to use a lot of them. I buy few packaged or processed foods, and use lots of house brands. I shop where my card allows me to benefit from all the store coupons without needing to clip them. This is a real plus, since whenever

I tear out in-store coupons, the item number is missing, and the cashier treats me like a thief.

Actually, collecting coupons can generate lots of tension. Do you rip them out of the paper or neatly cut them out? Few questions so divide people. Some individuals insist on neatly cutting them out, even when they realize no one else is going to be reading the paper. I am of the ripping school, and have a theory that people who neatly cut out their coupons are also highly likely to intensely dislike call waiting, though this is a subject for another book.

Whatever I save in coupons is probably offset by my instinct to purchase items in too large a quantity. After all, my son, Mike, didn't nickname me Mr. Bulk for nothing.

Once at Sam's Club I bought a GIGANTIC package of pinto beans, maybe five or six bucks' worth. I put them all up to soak at the same time, using all my big pots. When I started storing them in containers, I quickly noticed two things. My freezer was getting full, and I was running out of Tupperware. I flipped out, and threw half the beans away. Fortunately, I was able to foist the remainder onto my pinto bean-loving barber across the street.

I also had some cheese tension. I always buy the very large can of nacho cheese at Sam's. I use some of it, but the remainder usually spoils. One year I did a really smart thing. I was invited to a Super Bowl party, and graciously volunteered to bring my opened can of delicious nacho cheese. This worked out great. The nachos were a hit, and the cheese spoiled in my friend's fridge.

Be aware, however, that cost-effective shopping is undermined if you neglect to transfer everything in your cart into your car. Once I was shopping at Sam's and purchased a pound of smoked salmon (lox) for about ten bucks. But they don't have bags there, and the thin package of lox was laying loose in my cart with seven or eight other items. I loaded everything else into the car, but missed the lox. When I arrived home, I noticed I didn't have it.

I was mortified. I drove back to Sam's, but alas, I couldn't find my lox in any of the carts in the parking lot. I should have gone home and poured myself a beer. But in my frenzy, I actually entered the store and inspected carts, even those in use. For a split second, I came embarrassingly close to calling the authorities and requesting the first lox-APB in police history.

I've been ashamed of the thought ever since.

FREDDY'S TOP EIGHT SHOPPING POINTS

- The other grocery line ceases to move quickly the instant YOU enter it.

- Institutional sizes are for institutions.

- The time to send in the rebate form is the instant you arrive home from the store.

- The bigger the coupon clutch, the slower the checkout.

- Express lane shoppers who pay by check should be assessed a ten per cent surcharge.

- Don't assume that big product displays at the ends of aisles (known as endcaps) are bargains.

- Only look at the INSIDE of a tabloid once a month.

- It's ironic that vegetables spoil but Dove bars don't.

Fear
of
Frying

Salad Daze

Even though I was overweight, I had always loved salads. And I was spoiled. My wife's salads inevitably looked like mini-rainbows, with combinations of color and texture that prompted taste buds to send thank-you notes.

But when I sat down in my single-dad apartment to enjoy my first salad, I was in for a surprise. Nothing was on the table! Salads, apparently, didn't appear by magic.

Such was my introduction to the realities of food preparation. I was shocked to learn that cukes didn't come sliced, and that whole carrots didn't come peeled. Nor do fruits and vegetables show up on their own in the vegetable bin, and march under their own power onto a gaily decorated salad plate.

I imagined food preparation would be like the cooking shows on television, where skilled chefs quickly prepare complex dishes. I never thought about the shopping, and slicing and dicing by assistants, before the cameras start rolling. All the chefs do is dump the ingredients into a bowl. Unfortunately, in my house, gravity didn't cut it!

My initial salads were terribly inferior. Perhaps they weren't even technically salads, since they merely consisted of a few pieces of lettuce. More often than not, the leaves were partly brown. Lacking cukes and mushrooms to cover the worst spots, I improvised, using lots of dressing for ground cover.

My friends didn't always stoically acquiesce in their lettuce-torture. Inexplicably, they expected their greens to be green. "Is this the color they're showing this week?" George asked, eyeing his rust-colored side dish. Chuck at least eschewed sarcasm and stressed practicality. "Fred, do you want sixty-nine cents for a fresh head?"

Eventually, my repertoire expanded, and I'm actually now a seven-item salad guy: lettuce, green peppers, mushrooms, cukes, cherry tomatoes, and croutons. That's only six, because I saved the nicest touch for last. I grate a few bite-sized carrots over each salad plate. It's a pretty effect that women especially love.

I also often use a wonderful salad dressing, which I learned about from my friend Paula. Here's the recipe for Paula's Great Dressing:

Combine a quarter cup of both apple cider vinegar and sugar, one-third of a cup of salad oil, two tablespoons of chopped green onions, and two cloves of minced garlic. Add one teaspoon of dill seed, celery seed, and salt, along with one-quarter teaspoon of pepper and oregano.

You can prepare this several hours ahead of time, and I'm confident your guests will all love it. Be advised that the vinegar and sugar separate, so in a salad bottle the dressing looks a little scary. When serving, give the salad bottle a vigorous shake, and enjoy!

Unfortunately, my early salad success went to my head, and I sought out new taste and texture treats at an absurd pace. Once I prepared a salad consisting solely of vegetables I had never eaten: swiss chard, kohlrabi, kale, turnips, and rutabaga. Unfortunately, I forgot my boys were coming over for dinner that evening.

"What's this?" Bob asked, as I put the plate down in front of him. "A salad," I responded. "How was your day?" I asked, trying to divert his attention. "Better than this mess," he shot back. Then Mike joined in. "What's in here?" he inquired, giving the salad his best death stare. I confessed.

That's when the sarcasm really got heavy. "Ruta what?" Mike asked. "Baga," I said. "It's a kind of turnip." "Right," Mike said. "I remember now. A rooty baggie a day keeps the doctor away!"

Then Bob started in. "Swiss chard. It's a sort of leafy weed. I'll bet it outsells real lettuce ten-to-one! Dad, all these new things are so tasty," he continued, "it's surprising you served salad dressing."

Despite their reactions, I cleaned my plate and was better for the adventure, even though these vegetables won't soon put cukes and bell peppers out of business. The boys, however, weren't as venturesome, and hardly took a bite. I made a mental note never to serve them a salad with two ingredients starting with the letter "K."

As I spent more and more time in produce sections, I became far more quality conscious. Once I needed a green pepper, yet none in the bin looked appetizing. Each one was horribly wrinkled or mushy. In a former day, I'd have bought the first one I grabbed. But this time I asked to speak to the produce manager. Voilà! He immediately brought out fresh peppers from storage.

Quality was more sporadic when I purchased fruits or vegetables in sealed packages. Once I brought home a container of cherry tomatoes. The top row consisted of round wonders, perfect aero-

UNSAFE ON ANY BURNER

bic specimens. The middle row was filled with mediocre tomatoes trying to show pride despite spoilage. The bottom row consisted of soft little rejects. Was this layout a coincidence? I think not!

As I became more and more of a produce maven, I changed my buying habits. Initially I always bought the largest cucumbers I could find. Why not? The big ones were the same price as the small ones. But then I discovered the disadvantage of big cukes: they have seeds the size of Saturn. So now the smaller ones do quite fine, thank you.

In fact, I once helped out an obviously "lost" male shopper. He was working off of a list, and I just sensed that his wife had sent him out to do a little last-minute holiday shopping. The guy walked up to the cucumber bin, and did exactly what I had done previously: selected the two largest he could find (men!). I approached the gentleman. After assuring him that he could buy whatever he wanted, I suggested that his wife might instead prefer the smaller cukes.

But then the situation got a little tense. Turns out he was with his wife. He went over to the meat department, told her of our conversation, and he walked to me with HER. "Tell me again what to do," he said.

I was getting nervous. Regretted intervening. I repeated my advice to the woman. Whew—she agreed with me. What a relief! I felt proud that I knew enough to be helpful, but now try just to give advice to individuals shopping by themselves.

I am also a more skillful potato shopper. I used to buy the ten pound bags on sale. At the time, they seemed like a great buy. But I'd always waste a lot. Further, many of the potatoes in these bags are small, and are more difficult to peel than the larger potatoes I now buy individually.

Plus, my potato buddies almost cost me a heart attack. In my rookie days, I once put a bag of potatoes in a cabinet, and forgot about it. Five months later when I opened the cabinet I was attacked by dozens of man-eating sprouts. I had never seen anything like it! Long vines enveloped my being. In my shock, it took a moment to figure out what was happening. A minute more, and I would have dialed 9-1-1! Thankfully, I escaped, and resolved to keep potatoes in the fridge where I could keep a better eye on them.

Because I really like fresh salads, I spend a lot of time in produce sections. Despite all these visits, I have never quite reconciled myself to the enormous week to week price fluctuations. Once my local paper printed a great sounding recipe for asparagus soup. So I became an asparagus buyer for the first time, and paid ninety-nine cents for a pound. The soup was terrific.

UNSAFE ON ANY BURNER

Three weeks later I wanted to make it again, and stopped at the store to buy my asparagus. But I was floored. The very same pound of asparagus was $2.99. "That can't be right," I said to myself. I sought out an employee. "There's a wrong price on the asparagus," I said.

The clerk checked the sign. "That's correct," he said. "It's $2.99 a pound." "But it was $.99 a pound three weeks ago," I countered. "That's an interesting historical perspective," he replied. "But all that concerns us now is today's price, which is $2.99 a pound."

I was flabbergasted. How could a price triple in three weeks? "What caused this?" I asked the clerk. "Were all the asparagus pickers kidnapped? Did smugglers hijack an asparagus convoy?"

The clerk had no answers. "I just work here, sir. The price is $2.99. I have to get back to work," he said, starting to walk away. "This is ridiculous," I said. "I'll pay $2.19." "What?" the clerk said, walking back toward me. "I'll pay $2.19 for a pound," I repeated. "We don't negotiate," the incredulous clerk responded. "Okay," I said. "Final offer, $2.29!" He didn't bite. "Mister," he said, walking away, "$2.99, take it or leave it!" Since I had a guest arriving in three hours that expected asparagus soup, I took it.

Swallowing my pride at least had one advantage:

I shortly got to swallow the soup. Here's the recipe for Unbelievable Asparagus Soup:

Saute over medium heat two ounces of sesame seeds in two tablespoons of olive oil. After about four minutes, add one medium onion, and then two washed and cubed medium baked potatoes. Cook about five minutes. Add a pound of cleaned asparagus, broken into pieces. Add two cups water, and one-quarter teaspoons of both black pepper and ground nutmeg. Bring to boil, and then simmer approximately twenty minutes. Place in blender, and puree till soup is consistency you desire. Garnish with yogurt, sour cream, and/or croutons. This tastes GREAT.

Of course getting vegetables home (regardless of price) is one thing. Successfully forming them into a salad is another.

My true dicing education began one day when I was cooking with my friend Susan. A recipe called for two ribs of cut-up celery. We each took a rib, and did our thing. When she was finished she looked up and discovered I was but a third through.

She burst out laughing. "You cut like a novice," she said. "I am a novice," I replied. "Didn't your mother teach you anything?" she asked. "Leave my mother out of this," I replied, testily.

After Susan settled down, she taught me how to dice. With celery, cut the rib lengthwise into three

UNSAFE ON ANY BURNER

sections. Then, when you cut crosswise, you're creating three pieces with every cut.

On a washed and seeded green pepper, cut almost a full strip, but leave just a bit of the piece attached to the body of the pepper. Do this repeatedly across the entire side. Then turn the pepper ninety degrees, and repeatedly cut across it.

Onions were always a special challenge, since my eyes get quite teary. Susan suggested that running cold water minimizes the problem, but this never seemed to make much of a difference to me. One thing I did (painfully) learn. When your eyes tear, don't rub them with your fingers; they've been IN the onions. Reach instead for the comfort of a wet washcloth.

Of course buying produce is one thing, eating it is another. Are you a produce waster? I am, and I'm not alone. I polled twenty homemakers, male and female. Most confided they throw out about thirty per cent of the produce they buy. The real issue, therefore, isn't the cost of the produce we buy, but whether we actually use it.

Of course the hectic pace of our lives contributes to this phenomenon. We buy a lettuce with good intentions, only to eat out the following three evenings. And it seems vegetables have a way of disappearing in the fridge; my green peppers instinctively know to hide behind the o.j.

Signs in produce sections also contribute to waste.
"Corn, 10 for $1.00." "Cukes, 2 for $.98." As far as
I've discovered, there is never a meaningful volume discount in the produce department. Yet when
we see these signs, we sometimes turn into sheep,
and buy more than we need.

Once I approached a lady buying a mountain of
oranges. "Mam," I said. "I'm just curious. How
many oranges did you come in for?" She was taken
aback, but was willing to tell me. "I came in for
four," she said. I then counted the oranges in her
cart. "I see that you're buying ten. Can I ask why?"
She proudly pointed to the sign, "10 for $1.99."

"You can of course buy as many oranges as you
want," I said. "But do you know what you're saving by buying the six extra oranges?" She had no
idea. So I told her. Individual oranges cost twenty
cents. By buying ten, she was saving a PENNY!
When she realized the limited extent of her savings, she put back six of her oranges!

Of all my produce, I waste the fewest apples and
carrots. These both seem to stay fine in the refrigerator for upwards of two weeks. I've resolved to
buy more of these, to cut my waste. And if I have
half a cuke, I never return it to the vegetable bin. I
leave it visible on a refrigerator shelf, as a reminder
to eat it.

Recently I had a unique encounter with my vegetable bin. I discovered a nasty smell in my refrigerator, which I traced to the general area of the vegetable bin. Even with a horrible cold, my nose revolted the instant I opened the refrigerator door. Concerned, I painstakingly sniffed every vegetable in the vegetable bin, but could not find the problem. So I pitched everything, which killed me, as many of these fruits and vegetables were newly purchased.

Next day I made a special trip to my grocer and restocked. But after loading the fresh fruits and vegetables into the bin, the smell was still there! "Why do I keep buying spoiled produce?" I asked myself. Once again I emptied the bin and bought fresh. But when I discovered the stench was STILL there, I sought assistance.

I knocked on Mary's door and desperately pleaded for help. She returned with me to my apartment, and removed the vegetable bin. "Aha!" she said, gazing at the bottom of the refrigerator. As she thought, a spill from months previous was wreaking havoc. I cleaned and scraped for an hour, and soon had my fresh smelling fridge (and bin) back.

As I recall this incident, I truly regret needlessly discarding so much good produce. But at least I learned a valuable lesson from my bin caper: maximizing one's produce investment is sometimes a matter of both dollars AND scents.

FREDDY'S TOP EIGHT SALAD POINTS

- The lettuce discarded in most households could feed ten thousand bunnies.

- Paring knives are for more than pears.

- Don't pay more than a thousand dollars for a yellow or orange bell pepper.

- The produce manager always has fresher produce in the back room.

- If God wanted us to eat rooty baggies, he would have given us longer ears and a cotton tail.

- Your children will always request the one variety of salad dressing you don't have.

- Buying produce in bulk makes little sense if there is no volume discount.

- The nutritional benefits come from EATING vegetables, not just buying them.

One Cook Can
Spoil the Broth

As I travelled up the cooking learning curve, numerous guests suffered unspeakable indignities. Not even premium ingredients could make up for my lack of skill. I used Softasilk cake flour, but the dessert was hard as a rock. My "Constant Comment" brought frequent rebuke. Even when I used "Applause," I still heard, "I Can't Believe It's Not Tasty."

Much of my cooking ineptitude can be traced to my sheer lack of experience. But I'll tell you this: once you make a blunder, you remember it forever.

My poor son Mike suffered through one of my earliest disasters. I was preparing spaghetti, and believe it or not, I had never before made it. Back when I was in college, doing my limited cooking, pasta was not yet king.

But I had asked around, and was fairly certain I was up to the task. I bought some hamburger meat, and fried it to perfection. I whisked it off the burner the second the last hint of pink disappeared. But no one ever told me the obvious, that I needed to drain off the fat. This was mistake number one.

Unfortunately, more were to come. Of course I needed to heat the spaghetti sauce (needless to say, I bought prepared). The label on the jar indicated that the sauce should be heated at a low temperature. Since I had neglected to start cooking the sauce when I should have, I figured I'd warm it on medium. I allowed the sauce to cook while I joined Mike for conversation in the living room.

Five minutes later, when I went back into the kitchen to check on my meal, I was greeted with spaghetti sauce flying all over the place. It was on the stovetop. On the ceiling. On the floor. On the refrigerator. I now believe it was spaghetti sauce, not volcanic eruptions, that really did in Vesuvius and Pompeii.

Like a good homemaker, I wiped off what I could. But I couldn't reach the gunk on the ceiling. To this day it remains there. If a guest makes inquiries, I pass it off as an avant-garde stencil.

Thus far I was zero for meat, zero for spaghetti sauce. I couldn't destroy the noodles, could I? Fortunately they cooked up fine, but I had a problem getting them out of the pot. Because these were my early days, I hadn't yet purchased tongs, and didn't yet know I needed a colander. Today if this happened, I would attempt to skillfully use the top of the pot to hold back the noodles while I drained the water out. But I didn't think like this then.

All I knew is that I had innocent noodles drowning before my very eyes. So Mike and I attempted to lift them out of the water by manipulating a "shovel" consisting of a pancake flipper in one hand and potato masher in the other. As we would successfully lift up a few noodles, we'd hold them above the pot for a moment, to allow them to drain. Inevitably, we couldn't maintain the delicate balance long enough, and many now-irritated noodles returned to the pot for a needless additional soaking.

Eventually we were able to lure enough noodles out. But their relief was short lived, for they were immediately covered with my grease-ridden spaghetti sauce. Mike was a sport, and we both managed to eat half our portions. From this experience I learned to respect printed instructions, and not to venture far from a stove in use.

Mike experienced the brunt of another disaster. In my single-dad apartment, I was using a folding table as my dining room table. It was terribly unstable. I was making the boys one of my best meals ever, steak and baked potatoes and salad. I even made a special trip to the store for flowers and A-1 steak sauce.

I had served the boys steaks before, but had received complaints the meat was tough. Perhaps their mother uses a better butcher. In any event, I presented the sirloin steaks to my boys, and immediately heard the "tough" complaint. Mike even said they were "impossible to cut." I didn't own steak knives, so I told him simply to slice harder.

But because the table was unstable, the motion of his cutting caused the open bottle of A-1 steak sauce AND the flower vase to fall simultaneously. As luck would have it, they both landed on Mike's plate, and absolutely drowned his steak!

I learned two things from the A-1 affair. Buy higher quality meat, and invest in steak knives.

Main courses, however, weren't alone in enduring my foibles. Fruits and vegetables suffered through two extraordinary blunders. The first involved the simple apple. I had read how easy it is to prepare baked apples. This intrigued me; not only are they delicious, but they give a quasi-gourmet appearance. When I saw an apple corer in the gadget aisle at my supermarket, I bit, and also bought brown sugar and cinnamon. The idea was to use the corer to excavate a hole in the apple, and then stuff in as much brown sugar and cinnamon as possible.

Since my two boys were coming over for dinner, I needed a total of three apples. But just to be on the safe side, I bought five, in case I flunked coring. Well, I'm not a handy guy. The first time I tried it, I was super aggressive and managed to put a hole through the bottom of the apple within two seconds. This ruined it, as I could see that the brown sugar and cinnamon would run out of the apple during the baking process. "Calm down Fred," I said to myself, as I reached for the next victim.

This time I manipulated the corer much more deftly, and stopped halfway through the apple. But wanting the best for my kids, I decided to drill deeper, so the maximum amount of brown sugar and cinnamon could be inserted. I was not content, and thought that I could probe an additional millimeter without sacrificing structural integrity. Wrong! My next mini-shove on the corer produced hole number two.

At this point I was down to just two apples, since I had eaten one on the way home from the market. So I chalked it up to experience, and ate the remaining apples on the spot. At dinner, when the boys asked why there was no dessert, I proudly said, "Today we're eating healthy."

The lesson I learned that day? Not to try for perfection the first time I make a dish.

My second produce incident involves burned portabella mushrooms. Martha and I had been dating about three months, and she arranged a barbecue at her place, so that I could meet her parents for the first time. She had advised me that Wally, her dad, was a vegetable lover, and took great delight in the proper preparation of healthy appetizers.

When I shook hands with Wally, he informed me he had purchased portabella mushrooms from a stand down the road, some of the largest and most beautiful he had ever seen. "I love them barbecued," he said. I was the barbecuer, and forced a smile. But I was crying on the inside. As I've indicated, I'm a lousy barbecuer.

Well, I carefully placed Wally's wonder mushrooms on the hibachi, but made a rookie mistake, putting them too close to the fire. A short while later I learned I had erred when Wally asked, "Were you trying to burn my mushrooms?" I apologized profusely, and offered to drive to the stand to buy replacements. He thanked me, but insisted on going himself so he could purchase only the choicest.

He brought back three more, and wished me good luck at the grill. This time I placed them further from the flame, but unfortunately got distracted because some of the younger people present were playing basketball. I love the game, and couldn't resist the opportunity to join them. Never have I played so well. Every shot went in. Clearly I was NBA material. I was absolutely on fire. Unfortunately, so were the portabellas.

I sheepishly announced my second failure, and offered to go buy thirds. Wally fortunately decided to cut his losses, and made do with the rutabaga Martha was preparing. He treated me cordially the rest of the evening, but never again allowed me near fresh produce. And for the ten months Martha and I dated, he always referred to me as the "Mushroom Kid."

Of course, I now realize how quickly vegetables can burn. So if I see a basketball game, I wait until after dinner to play.

Throughout my misadventures with vegetables, at least my safety was never in question. Not so with the high calorie dessert I made for my boys. I saw the recipe in the paper; a reader had requested it after an especially satisfying experience in a local restaurant.

Gosh, the dish, Lemon-Lime Pie, sounded good. It had two layers. Each consisted of a can of sweetened condensed milk, an eight ounce cream cheese, eight ounces of whipped topping, and either lemon or lime juice. And it looked easy.

I had never before worked with sweetened condensed milk, so I had trouble finding it in the store. But when I did, I was shocked by how many calories it has, about thirteen hundred in fourteen ounces. And this dessert called for two cans.

This got me counting. What with the two cream cheeses, the two whipped toppings, and the crust, this dessert was approaching six thousand calories. But for the boys, why not?

Unfortunately, I encountered a rookie problem when I made it. I creamed together one can of the milk with one of the cream cheeses, but neglected to fold in one container of topping before putting the mixture in the pie shell. Nowadays, this would be no problem. I'd just fold it in right then and there. But I was still a rookie, and wanted to do things right. I attempted to take the mixture out of the pie shell, but tore the bottom of it.

"So what?" you're saying. "It's on the bottom. Who cares?" But I was inexperienced, and thought I had ruined it. I decided to start over from scratch, but first I'd have to go out and purchase another cream cheese and can of sweetened condensed milk.

This time I went to a different market, and a young, courteous employee told me where to find the milk. But I was still seething at my stupidity in bungling the recipe. "You stupid idiot," I said to myself.

UNSAFE ON ANY BURNER

Well, the employee who helped me heard this, even though I assumed he was out of earshot. And he was six-five, and about four hundred pounds. "Who are you calling an idiot?" he asked, fists clenched. I mumbled something about "myself" and departed as quickly as possible.

Of course, the boys loved the dessert, but it was WAY too sweet. We each could only eat the thinnest of slices. I gave them the leftovers to take home, and half suspect they threw the pie away, although I haven't worked up the courage to ask.

Now I know that I should have read the recipe more closely before committing myself to make it. It was obvious the dessert was going to be too rich. I've also learned to monitor the position of store employees who cross my path.

Common sense should have helped me avoid some of my misadventures. But I seem to bear out the saying, "Common sense is not so common." Consider these three incidents:

I learned of a FANTASTIC garnishing idea for orange juice. Please, please try it. Merely put the o.j. in a blender, and turn it on for several seconds. The orange juice develops a head, a froth, that makes it lighter and tastier. Especially if you are having guests for brunch, orange juice like this really looks elegant in a pitcher. And kids LOVE it.

Well, I was so proud of discovering this "trick," I

called my kids into the kitchen to witness me prepare my "magic" orange juice. I filled the pitcher
of the blender almost all the way to the top, and
turned on the machine. Instantly I had orange juice
running all over my floor.

"What's happening?" I yelled. Then I discovered
the problem. Air was increasing the volume of the
orange juice, and as a result, the blender couldn't
contain it. If I had any common sense, I would have
known this would occur.

Blunder number two took even more stupidity.
And it shows that I'm not kidding: I DO lack common sense.

The first few times I prepared chicken soup, I
struggled. Seemingly, I didn't do a good job of
skimming off the fat. I recall my wife standing over
a soup pot, removing teaspoons-full of fat. Yet
when I immersed my spoon in the pot, all I seemed
to capture was broth.

Then I read a "tip" in the newspaper. If I added
ice cubes to the pot, the fat would congeal around
them. Bingo, no more fat problems. So I put some
water in my rarely used ice cube trays, shoved them
back into the freezer, and waited with anticipation
to try my new "insider" technique.

I prepared my next chicken soup with particular
care. Diced with extra precision. Purchased an especially enticing bird. And at the proper moment,

I proudly added the two magical ice cubes. But there was a problem. I added them to my BOIL-ING soup. Rather than capturing my fat, the cubes instantly melted, diluting my wonder broth. Clearly, the cubes only help if they are put in the soup after it has cooled, but the "tip" didn't say THAT.

Finally, there was the "Chicken Portion Caper." Bob was coming over for dinner. For one of the few times, I bought a prepared meal for him, a Wonder Roast chicken from my local market. I only purchased one, as I had eaten a late lunch and didn't think I'd be hungry.

Let me fess up to a bad habit. I sometimes consume food bought for my boys before they actually arrive. This is especially true for the baguette I buy for garlic bread when I make spaghetti. The more traffic lights I stop at, the more pieces I eat. I often complain to my guys that bakeries shouldn't be allowed to sell half-loaves, but they see right through it.

Unfortunately, I found myself hungrier than I expected. Bob wasn't due for twenty minutes, so I tore off one of the chicken's wings. "He won't notice it," I confidently predicted. But then the other wing started flirting with me. "I should eat it," I said. "If the chicken has just one wing, Bob will be suspicious." And after that I downed a drumstick.

Please understand, this was a small chicken to begin with. I put the remaining carcass on a smaller plate, to make it appear bigger. And I substituted a smaller place mat for the normal one, for similar effect. I stretched out the remaining chicken pieces as best I could, hoping to cover at least a fair percentage of the new, smaller plate.

But alas, Bob was not fooled. He knew his father too well. He walked in, took a quick look at the table, and headed for the kitchen. He returned with a bowl of Special K and one question: "Did you enjoy my chicken?"

FREDDY'S TOP EIGHT
COOKING DISASTER POINTS

- Tis better to brown and serve than burn and discard.

- When passing off store-bought food as home-made, remember to remove the price sticker.

- Jello is NOT an entree.

- If the cake fails, blame the altitude.

- Man can live by bread alone, but it's no fun.

- When preparing grilled cheese, take the slice of cheese out of the plastic wrapper prior to cooking.

- If at first you d

- It helps to have

OMG!

You Cook in That Kitchen?!!!

As you might suspect, regular cleaning was NOT my priority. In fact, it's only lately that I've learned that supermarkets actually have "Cleaning Aisles."

Let me paint you a picture of the early days in my apartment. The kitchen floor was a literal mosaic of spills. "Was the spaghetti sauce tasty?" Marcia inquired, reading my floor like an experienced tracker. "Why'd you overcook your broccoli?" Sue asked, deciphering a recent arrival.

The floor mosaic continued on the appliances. I rarely cleaned the inside of the refrigerator. Occasional spills there didn't concern me; "they'll evaporate," I said. And anything solid would eventually biodegrade.

UNSAFE ON ANY BURNER

And my stove...well, let's just say my stove was in no danger of becoming the cover-model for *Modern Appliance* magazine. In particular, the broiling pan was a disgrace. I frequently baked chicken, one of the few things I knew how to prepare. But I had the horrible habit of usually letting the broiler pan sit for about a week before cleaning it. And inevitably the pan was not in the stove but on top of it, or on the floor (yes, the floor). So whenever I came home from work, my poor nostrils were assaulted by chicken potpourri.

My dishwashing was also suspect. Initially my concept of cleanup was burning the paper plates. Unfortunately, I discovered I greatly preferred the real thing, as did my guests.

But often I couldn't prepare the food I wanted because a required, still-dirty pot was inaccessible, buried beneath tons of dishware. And when I finally did excavate the desired piece, great effort was needed to clean it. More often than not, the cereal had turned into cement, or the spaghetti sauce stains were impregnable. Exhausted from the cleanup, I'd put the dishes away wet, hoping evaporation would do its thing before my next meal.

This extraordinary disorder in my kitchen created more than one crisis. Once on a trip to San Francisco years earlier, I had bought a lovely set of six petite porcelain soup spoons. They weren't out-rageously valuable, but they held a great deal of sentimental value.

After one of my first dinner parties, I could only locate five of the spoons. Where was the sixth? I checked the floor under the dining room table, with no success. I decided to inspect the pile of dirty dishes stacked in my sink. Negative.

At this point I was motivated enough to begin washing the dishes. But as I did so, the drain clogged, and water began backing up. I instinc-tively turned on the garbage disposal.

The noise was deafening! I knew at once what was happening. The disposal was destroying my spoon. I instantly turned it off, but the damage was done. My recovered spoon now was in three pieces. But I learned a good lesson. Whenever anything smaller than a coffee cup is missing, check the dis-posal.

The lack of order created a similar incident with a fondue fork. I had eight in all, and frequently liked to serve fondue. But I suddenly became aware I could only locate seven. Because I was hosting eight for fondue in a week, I intensified my search.

Remembering the soup spoon catastrophe, I checked the disposal, and came up empty. I searched EVERY cabinet, to no avail. Finally I had to call one of the guests and ask him to bring his

UNSAFE ON ANY BURNER

set.

Nine months later, the mystery was solved. I have a large, rectangular container in one of my kitchen cabinets, where I throw my spare change. After eleven months it was at last full. The container was quite heavy, and I expected a windfall.

At the bank I carefully handed my treasure-trove to the teller. He disappeared with it in the back room, and soon I heard the familiar clatter of the tabulating machine. I kept hoping the distinctive noise would never cease. After a lengthy period I heard the last "Clink."

The teller returned promptly, with a big smile. I assumed he had good news for me. But I was surprised as he described my windfall. "Congratulations Mr. Gosman," he said. "You get back two hundred and fifty dollars and forty cents, plus seven paper clips, a Monopoly house, and one twelve-inch fondue fork!"

Given the disorder in my kitchen, you can understand why I tried to keep women out of it. When a friend arrived for dinner, I would whisk her quickly into the living room. After dinner I would routinely do the clearing, urging my guest to make herself comfortable on the couch.

Unfortunately, the living room was far from pristine itself. For the first two months in my apartment, I lacked both a vacuum and a rake. I was tempted to rent a leaf blower, and blow out the debris, but I didn't have a sliding door.

Things were so bad, my friend Paula embarrassed me into a cleanup. She dropped by to pick me up for a walk one day, and she was appalled. "Don't you EVER clean your baseboards?" she asked. Up to that point, I hadn't even known I had baseboards.

Since she was coming over the following Friday to celebrate her birthday, I decided to surprise her with clean baseboards. I got on my hands and knees with a wet rag, and went all around my apartment, attacking the dusty buildup with abandon. But I took a short cut, and only dusted the baseboards that were visible. Why bother with anything else?

Unfortunately, an amazing thing happened that evening. Paula was using the phone, which rests atop the television. While she was speaking, the base unit fell BEHIND the TV. "I'll get it," I quickly volunteered, hoping to prevent Paula from going on a dust witch hunt. "Don't bother," Paula replied. "I dropped it; I'll pick it up."

Since the television was close to the wall, freeing the object was not at all simple. Paula was on her knees, awkwardly stretching to reach it. When she finally freed it, the unit was covered with a neglected baseboard's worth of dust. Paula smiled at the time, and headed to the table like a lady to enjoy dessert and open her present. But to this day she makes phone calls at HER house.

My women friends generally understood that I absolved them of any responsibility for the state of my apartment. Therefore, they were usually quite relaxed when other couples joined us for dinner. Jessica, however, was the exception. Her home was always immaculate, and she didn't approve of my housekeeping. "How can you entertain guests in an apartment that looks like this?" she asked.

I tried to put her fears to rest, but she was insistent. "The bathroom mirror is FILTHY," she said. She requested five minutes for touch up. "No way," I said. "This is your night out." But as she repeated her plea, tears welled up in her eyes. "Okay," I said. And she forbade me to assist.

As she raced for the bathroom, I retrieved the timer. She first scrubbed down the mirror. "Isn't that better?" she asked. I nodded, although I saw no difference. "Four minutes," I announced. She then refolded the hand towels, and poured more liquid soap into the soap dispenser. "A full soap dispenser gives a more pleasant appearance," she advised. I gave her a nod, and an update, "Two minutes."

She then noticed the built-in soap dish, and was horrified. "Why this hasn't been washed in years!" she exclaimed. She grabbed the nearest clean wash cloth and started rubbing furiously. "Fifty seconds," I called out. The hardened stains resisted her passionate strokes. Around the fifteen second mark, disaster struck. She was rubbing SO hard, the ancient soap dish broke into three pieces.

She apologized profusely. "I'm so sorry," she said. "I don't know how this happened." I told her to forget about it, and thanked her for trying. But the next time she came over, she brought TWO things: a bottle of Merlot for us, and Crazy Glue for the bath.

Two incidents transformed me into a better home-maker. Once I prepared a delicious steak for Jessica. I really went overboard. Bought a choice cut. Proudly sprinkled on my newly bought garlic powder. Even sauteed mushrooms, for the first time. But when I served the steak, I placed it on the first dish I pulled out from my cabinet. Unfortunately, it still had a quarter inch of water on it from a recent washing. So Jessica ate MY steak, while I had to make do with soggy sirloin.

But the real eye-opener was the hummus incident. One day I spilled some hummus on my kitchen floor, and didn't clean it up (no surprise there). That night I had trouble sleeping, and went to the kitchen to prepare a snack. Barefoot, I stepped squarely in the middle of a tremendous mound of hummus. "What is this?" I said to myself, frantically groping in the dark for a paper towel. Later that day, while washing hummus tracks off my linoleum, I was born again.

I became a veritable dirt devil, a trash-hating, mini Mr. Clean. The first improvement was my garbage pail. I had purchased the wrong kind initially, as it lacked a top. My chicken potpourri was odoriferous enough for me, so I quickly bought the better kind.

I ATTACKED the kitchen floor. Actually got on my hands and knees, and scrubbed it with a brush. It positively shone! But I did encounter a funny situation whenever I washed it. Wanting to get it really clean, I would always fill my pail with an excessive amount of Pine Sol, maybe eight times what was needed. My kitchen smelled of it for days.

I began to promptly confront my dirty dishes. And I no longer put them away wet. I purchased three dish towels, and these proved fine for a time. But then a friend convinced me to try a drying rack. But the first time I used it, I embarrassed myself.

Truthfully, I wasn't sure how it worked. I guess I assumed water would drip off the plates and fall into the bottom of the rack for eventual evaporation. So when I used it the first time, I placed it haphazardly on the counter. While I was filling it with newly washed dishes, I noticed that my floor was getting sopping wet. It was then that I noticed that one of the sides of the rack was sloped, to allow water to drain into the sink! Now I always position the rack properly, and can't imagine anyone drying by hand when gravity can do the work.

Although I've improved my homemaking, I still have a lot to learn, as these following two incidents attest. One day while dusting I came upon a flower pot, with the cutest little flowers. I hadn't watered it since I had received it as a gift, about a month previous. I felt horrible about it, and gave it some water.

A week later, I was with Andrea, who had given me the little plant. I marvelled to her how hardy it was, surviving my inexcusable neglect. She started to laugh. "What's so funny?" I asked. "Nothing," she responded, "except it really isn't so surprising it survived. It's artificial!"

And then there was my battle with Mr. Coffee. There always seemed to be tough stains on the bottom of my clear coffee pot, since I usually only clean it when I make fresh coffee. And truthfully, not always then. So I squeezed a little dishwashing detergent in the pot, and scrubbed for a minute. Nothing happened. The stains didn't budge.

So I tried again. Same result. I decided to fill the pot with hot water and let it soak. But an hour later my efforts were similarly fruitless. "Perhaps I needed to use a stronger cleansing agent," I figured. So I squirted an extraordinary amount of liquid Soft Scrub into the pot, and vowed to return in an hour to show the repugnant receptacle who was boss.

Sixty-five minutes later the coffee pot looked the same, despite all my efforts. My frustration was mounting. I frantically knocked on Mary's door. Fortunately she was home, and I begged for assistance. After hearing my history of failure, she agreed to take the pot into her kitchen and give it a fresh try. So I left it with her, and trudged back to my apartment.

Forty seconds later there was a knock on my door. "Here's your pot," Mary said. I couldn't believe my eyes. There it was, spotless. For a second I thought she was playing a practical joke, substituting a similar-looking pot for mine.

"What did you do?" I asked, feeling more than a touch silly. "I rubbed hard," she said. "I did that, too," I quickly rejoined, convinced there must be some other explanation. "That you did," Mary said. "But you did it on the inside of the pot. I did it on the outside. That's where the stains were!"

FREDDY'S TOP EIGHT
CLEANLINESS POINTS

- Always clean your dishes in the same month they get dirty.

- Compulsively neat cooks rarely prepare Sloppy Joes.

- Never underestimate the amount of clutter a closed shower curtain can hide.

- The dirtier the stovetop, the bigger the spoon caddy.

- Dimming the lights is easier than dusting the baseboards.

- Sweep the crumbs off the dining room table BEFORE you vacuum.

- Your woman guest gets the cleanest place mat.

- You know your home requires cleanup if a thief ransacks it and it takes you two months to notice.

Serve No Thyme
Before Its Whine

When I started out, I was a spice idiot. Didn't know anything about them. If you'd have asked, I'd have said sage was advice, and rosemary, Clooney.

But, boy did I get an education when I cooked for my first guest! Mary, my neighbor, dropped in for dinner, and I made chicken breasts. "They look gorgeous," Mary said, smiling. "Chicken is my favorite."

Unfortunately, Mary's smile disappeared with her first bite. "Do these taste a little plain to you?" she asked. "Not at all," I said, "I love plain food." Mary gave me a look that said, "I can't believe you said that!" and braced for her next bite. After a painfully slow chew, her mood didn't improve.

I sensed the meal didn't meet with her favor. "Mary," I said, "I'm a rookie, and want to improve. If something isn't perfect, I want you to tell me." "Are you serious?" she asked. "I don't want to hurt your feelings." "Totally serious," I responded. But she wasn't yet one hundred per cent comfortable. "You're not going to get defensive?" she inquired. I promised not to.

"Then could I trouble you for rosemary?" she said. "For what?" I responded. "Rosemary," she repeated. "Mary," I said, "you're the only guest I invited. No one else is coming." "No, no, no," she responded. "Not rosemary the person, rosemary the spice." She went on to tell me all about it, and was disappointed when I informed her I didn't have any.

"Well then I'll just take some tarragon," she said. "Some what?" I said. "Tarragon, it's a spice," she said. "Uh-Oh," I said to myself. "Now I'm in more trouble." Since I was tarragon-less, I resorted to humor. "What kind of name is that for a woman?"

Mary was not amused. "I don't need tasteless jokes AND tasteless chicken," she said. She got up and briskly walked to her apartment. I feared our short friendship was over. Thankfully she returned shortly, smiling. She had with her jars of rosemary and tarragon, her favorite spices. She put them on the table, gave me a playful hug, and said, "NOW

UNSAFE ON ANY BURNER

we can eat chicken!"

She liberally sprinkled our chicken with her spicy treasures, and invited me to take a taste. I was amazed. "Wow! This is delicious," I said. Thus was born a spice-aholic.

That next day I visited two spice stores, and the spice aisle and produce section of my grocer. The variety just overwhelmed me. Hundreds of flavorings and seasonings from all over the world. I didn't have to travel to India or Thailand, for example, to eat food that tastes Indian or Thai; I could eat it in my own dining room. Between the spice shops and the grocer, I bought twenty-five (25!) different spices, and experimented with many of them.

My favorite turned out to be garlic. Fresh garlic is sold in a white bulb. Each bulb consists of twelve to eighteen cloves, and each clove has an outer skin that must be removed. Fresh garlic keeps for about a month, and should not be refrigerated.

But garlic has a problem. The cook needs to remove the outer skin from the clove, and this can be difficult, especially with short fingernails. The first time I tried to peel the skin off, I failed miserably. I kept trying to ensnare the skin, to rip it off, but I just couldn't do it.

But I wasn't a quitter, and, fork and knife flashing, decided to attack the clove in earnest. I stuck the fork securely into the clove's belly. I then took my sharp knife, and actually tried to slice off the skin. But with every cut, garlic came off also. By the time all the skin was removed, the sliver of garlic that remained was the diameter of a vermicelli.

So I tried again, with a new clove; failure was NOT an option. I muttered insults. "You're ugly and fat!" I said. "So are you," the clove responded. I stared at it with my famous "Evil Eye." After twelve minutes, as my headache became intolerable, Mary knocked on the door.

"What are you doing?" she asked. "Giving my garlic the 'Evil Eye,'" I proudly responded. Mary correctly sensed I had lost it, and took immediate corrective action. She grabbed a small glass, and carefully smashed the clove with it. "Look," she said. "Now the skin is easy to peel off." I didn't believe her. But when I inspected the clove, I could see that the glass had loosened the skin. I peeled it off in seconds.

Of course once garlic is skinless, it still must be minced. To accomplish this, you need a garlic press. Basically, a press squashes the garlic so that it's in tiny pieces. I would urge you to buy a good press, one that costs seven to fifteen dollars. The inexpensive ones are far less sturdy, and much less satisfying to work with.

One final point. If manipulating a garlic press is

difficult for you (some strength is needed), consider heating the cloves in the microwave for about twenty seconds. Not only does the skin peel off easily, but the warmed garlic minces effortlessly and the press is far easier to clean.

In addition to garlic, I also fell in love with cilantro. Have you ever tried it? It is a WONDER.

What do you do with cilantro? Add it to a salad, a sandwich, pasta, and just about anything to double your enjoyment. It is truly a marvel. If you haven't tried it, please do, and stay with it two or three times if you find the initial taste a tad unique. By the way, another name for cilantro is Chinese parsley.

Fresh cilantro can be found in the produce section of most any grocery store. It's sold in a bunch, like parsley. But you have to be careful when you buy it. You see, cilantro looks just like Italian parsley, and often is displayed right next to it. So you need to smell the cilantro, and absorb that incredible scent to confirm it's what you want (I'm having trouble describing the smell). Please ask an employee for assistance the first time you buy it. Trust me, you'll be happy you did.

Here's a FANTASTIC recipe for a simple dish featuring cilantro. It's called Freddy's Tex-Mex Wonder. Get out a large bowl. Dump in the following five ingredients, and with a big spoon mix them together. That's it.

Two cans of drained and rinsed black eyed peas. Two bunches of cut-up scallions including most of the stem. A cup and a half of medium or hot salsa. Six or more cloves of garlic (remembering to remove the skin!). And about half a bunch of cilantro, chopped up or simply torn into small pieces. Put Freddy's Tex-Mex Wonder on crackers, or stuff it into a pita, and you'll be in heaven. And for a few days it will keep very well in the refrigerator.

Speaking of wonders, I once thought Linda discovered an extraordinary spice when we were browsing in a spice shop. Boy, was I disappointed! The saleslady urged us to buy some epazote, a Mexican spice. "What does it do?" we asked. Clearly uncomfortable, the saleslady turned beet red. Linda and I were perplexed. What could be so embarrassing?

Suddenly the saleslady grabbed Linda and took her into a far corner of the store. The saleslady's look clearly communicated that I should stay put. Now I was really intrigued. I tried to listen in on their conversation, and could tell from Linda's expression she was getting an earful. Soon you could hear Linda's giggle all over the store. She returned excited and enthralled, and proceeded to buy two big bottles of epazote.

I immediately pumped Linda for details when

we left the store, but she acted embarrassed, and kept bringing up the weather. All the way home I kept probing. "Tell me! Tell me! What does it do?" My imagination was really piqued. What magic did these bottles contain?

Being male, I assumed epazote must be an aphrodisiac. What else could explain the saleslady's embarrassment and awkwardness (and why Linda bought two large jars)? But Linda played her hand well. I was chafing at the bit, riddled with curiosity, but she wasn't uttering syllable one. After extracting a promise that I'd wash her car AND take her to lunch, she fessed up. Turns out, epazote, when added to chili, apparently minimizes the effect of gas, if you understand what I'm trying to say. No WONDER Linda bought so much!

Fennel was another spice that fascinated me. I love its licorice taste. And I especially adore it on these Marvelous Won Ton Crackers, that are easy to make and go great with soup.

Here's what you do: Buy some won tons at the grocery. They are usually located near the produce or freezer section (if you buy frozen, let them defrost). Won tons usually measure three inches square. Cut them diagonally, and place them on a cookie sheet (re-form them into squares; you'll fit the most on). Brush each won ton with a mixture of olive oil and garlic. Sprinkle on Parmesan cheese and fennel seeds. Bake in a preheated four hundred degree oven for about six minutes, but watch them closely.

These are just wonderful! You'll love them. Allow them to sit for a minute or so after baking, as the crackers become even harder and crunchier as they cool. By the way, you don't need to grease the cookie sheet; the won tons don't stick, for reasons I don't understand. If you don't like fennel, substitute sesame or caraway seeds.

Food coloring was another little "extra" that enamored me. How can one little drop cause so much color change? But I committed a rookie error. A recipe called for green and yellow food coloring, so I went to the grocery store and purchased small bottles of each. Only later did I learn that food coloring is commonly sold in packages that have all four colors represented (red, green, blue, yellow).

Be careful with food coloring. The first time I used it, I was too cavalier, and got lots of green on me. I scrubbed and scrubbed, but the stain remained on my right hand. I fled to Mary's apartment, for advice and counsel. "What did you do?" she asked, gazing incredulously at my right hand. "Spilled some food color," I replied. She applied some Ajax, and scoured aggressively. But success eluded us. For two weeks I was embarrassed every time I shook hands. My only consolation was that with all the scrubbing, the green had transformed from kelly to citrus.

Speaking of color, I even became a zester. Zest has nothing to do with soap. Zest is the colorful, flavorful outside part of the peel, especially in lemons and oranges. To easily remove the zest, merely scrape the zester (a knife like gadget) along the skin of the fruit. The coveted zest easily falls off, and adds lots of flavor to your cooking.

A zester is well worth the money. It only costs about six bucks, and is far safer to use than a knife. Ask for a lemon zester—for some reason it's never called an orange zester.

As I became more and more intrigued with varied tastes, smells, and colors, I had trouble managing my burgeoning spice inventory. Jar after jar cluttered my apartment: some were on top of the fridge, some were in various cabinets, and some just sat out on the counters. It often took forever to find the specific spice I needed. I kept putting off getting organized until I ruined another chicken dinner for Mary.

One evening she came by and I again prepared chicken (remember, she loved it). I cooked it plain, but was confident I could satisfy her spice needs: I probably had fifty different varieties scattered around the house. Again she requested rosemary (the spice, not the person). "No problem," I said.

"I have a big jar."

But when I got up to look, I couldn't find it. I knew it was there. As I painstakingly searched the kitchen, Mary noticed my absence. "Everything okay in there?" she asked. "Piece of cake," I said. But shortly I had to admit defeat and confess I couldn't find her favorite spice.

She was a sport. "No problem, Fred," she said. "Just get me some tarragon." Hard to believe, the same problem recurred. I looked for ten minutes, but for the love of garlic, could not find it. I got so frustrated, I'd have paid a magician a hundred drachmas to turn my fenugreek into tarragon. I broke the bad news to Mary as gently as I could. Incredulous, she fled to her apartment to obtain the needed seasonings.

Tired of the déjà vu, Mary insisted on helping me organize my spices, and I was too embarrassed to refuse. We counted the spices and extracts, and they totalled forty-eight. She went with me to a hardware store, and we put up a large shelving unit in the kitchen, like the kind used in bathrooms to keep toiletries organized.

"Now we'll alphabetize," she said. "We'll what?" I responded. "Alphabetize," she repeated. "That's the only way to keep spices." "Why do it that way?" I asked. She was eloquent. "Fred, why spend precious minutes every time you cook looking for spices? I'm one of the least anal people around, but if you ask me for chili powder, I know I can find it between my chervil and my chives."

This made sense to me. But it took longer to organize the spices than I imagined. We'd fill the top row, but then need to move some of the jars to the second row to fit in an "A" or "C" in the first. We sometimes squabbled, differing, for example, on whether cayenne pepper was a "C" or a "P." But we usually smoothed things out, and after thirty minutes we had three and a half shelves full of meticulously alphabetized spices.

But then Mary ruined the evening. As she opened the refrigerator to get two celebratory brews, she noticed two spice jars still on top. "We have to add these to our shelves," she said. The first one was cumin, so we had to laboriously rearrange ALL the spices, moving some from the third row to the fourth, and second row to the third, to make room near the end of the first row for the additional "C." At this point I had worked forty minutes, and never wanted to see another spice jar again.

Then Mary reached for the remaining jar. "Rats," she said. It was another "C." We started to move all the jars once again, but suddenly I realized I had had enough. Over Mary's protests I took a deep breath, opened my garbage can, and proudly pitched my coriander!

FREDDY'S TOP EIGHT SPICE POINTS

- You can never add too much garlic.

- Thyme comes from the Greek word meaning "to fumigate."

- Basil was created to go with tomato.

- Cilantro is the leafy portion of the coriander plant.

- If you can't say Worchestershire Sauce, try "runny steak sauce."

- When you use food coloring, beware of green thumb syndrome.

- Generally add fifty per cent more of the extract (vanilla, lemon, etc.) than called for.

- The only way to organize spices is alphabetically.

When in Doubt,
Blame the Recipe

Afunny thing happened to me as I became creative in the kitchen: everything bombed. My "Zesty Cauliflower Surprise" evoked only yawns. And my "moist" cake, one that I slaved over all afternoon, turned out dry as the desert.

Unfortunately, my friends weren't shy in communicating their disappointment. "Boy, I'm glad I didn't supersize this," they'd say. Here I was, attempting to bravely spread my culinary wings, and my guests were giving me the bird. I called my friend, Linda, for consolation.

"Linda, everyone hates my cooking," I said. "Don't be ridiculous," she replied. Easy for her to say; she had declined two recent dinner invitations. "The best thing anyone said about my cauliflower was that it was white," I bemoaned. "And when I presented my cake, two guests said eating sand would have been preferable."

"They were probably just kidding," Linda said, not even trying to sound like she meant it. But concerned that I was about to enter a culinary Great Depression, she volunteered to come by the next day and observe the inept one in action.

When she arrived, I had all the ingredients laid out, and promptly started to prepare a simple casserole. Despite trying extra hard, I could tell my efforts were not impressing. As I closed the oven door on my casserole dish, Linda could contain herself no longer. "I've identified a problem," she said. "You don't do things in order. If there's seven ingredients to put in a bowl, you jump around, and go from number one, to seven, to two, to four. Just now you failed to put in number five. Work in order, Fred. This will solve most of your problems."

Linda had a point. Many of my dishes tasted as if something was missing. Now I knew why; something WAS missing!

I confided to Linda that one of my problems was that I was too literal. If a recipe called for a teaspoon of cinnamon, to me that meant exactly one teaspoon. I proudly measured some of the most level teaspoons in history.

Linda observed this literal side of me in action as

UNSAFE ON ANY BURNER

we made a soup together. The soup was supposed to simmer for thirty minutes. Exactly at twenty nine minutes and fifty nine seconds I was hovering over the pot, ready to whisk it from the burner.

"What are you doing, Fred?" she asked. "Preparing to take the pot off the burner," I replied. "The recipe said, 'Simmer thirty minutes.'" Linda looked bemused. "What do you think will happen if you leave the pot on a minute longer?" she asked.

I thought I'd answer quickly, but in truth I was stumped. "What would happen?" I asked myself. I considered various possibilities. The cookbook author might storm in and reclaim his opus. Not likely. The pot could burn. But it was just on simmer. "I guess nothing would happen," I finally said to Linda. "That's right," she said. "So relax!"

But mastering my compulsiveness proved a challenge. Once I went potato crazy at a local market. A cauliflower soup recipe called for a half pound of red potatoes. I weighed approximately twenty-five likely potatoes, but all were either a shade too light or too heavy.

I demanded to speak with the produce manager. Three minutes later he appeared; clearly I had interrupted him. "Do you have any half-pound red potatoes?" I asked (at the time it didn't seem like an idiotic question). "Pardon me," he responded. "Half-pound red potatoes," I repeated. "I need them for a soup recipe." He didn't appear amused. "Did you see our bin with two hundred red potatoes?" he asked. "Yes, but none is exactly a half pound." "What would you like me to do about it?" he asked. "Send a few to Weight Watchers?"

At this point I sensed he was losing interest in our conversation. I made do with the potato that was a sixteenth of a pound light, and the recipe forgave me.

Here is the recipe for Spicy Cauliflower Soup: In a little oil, saute for ten minutes a half-cup onion, two ribs of diced celery, and one diced carrot. Add a few tablespoons of water if the vegetables stick to bottom of pan. Add one and a half teaspoons of cumin, two teaspoons of curry powder, and one-quarter teaspoon of cayenne pepper. Stir thirty seconds. Add fourteen and a half ounces of low sodium chicken broth, and seventeen and a half ounces water. Put in one large cored and chopped cauliflower, and approximately one-half pound of unpeeled, chopped red potato. Bring to boil. Simmer about twenty to twenty-five minutes. Puree the soup in a blender. When done, mix in one tablespoon of lime juice. Serve garnished with vanilla yogurt and orange sections. Enjoy!

Despite Linda's help with the soup, I continued to stumble frequently. Once Linda discovered a two-sided recipe card, one that had recipes for both meatloaf and strudel. She thought I might want to try the strudel recipe, so she mailed it to me.

I was complimented, and swore I would apply the lessons she had taught me. I painstakingly followed each step, in exact order, and tried to relax and be less literal. But I made a slight goof when I looked at the two-sided recipe card to find out the strudel's baking time. Unknowingly I had turned it over, and gazed at the meatloaf's baking time. My strudel only needed fifteen to twenty minutes, but I put the poor thing in for an hour! Understandably, it was ruined.

Although incompetence like this was typically a burden, one time my stumbling and bumbling produced a culinary treasure. My unlikely discovery occurred when I was making my boys a cheesecake. I have unusual tastes in cheesecake—I prefer it plain, with nothing on top; and I love it heavy. Almost every cheesecake I eat isn't heavy enough.

I bought a box of Honey Maid Graham Cracker Crumbs, and for the first time I made a graham cracker crust from scratch (it's easy). Merely combine one and a quarter cups of graham cracker crumbs with one-quarter cup of sugar and one-third cup of melted butter or margarine. Press it down to cover the bottom of a springform pan (a special pan with removable sides).

But when I made the cheesecake, I neglected to

put in the required cup of sour cream. I wasn't even aware of my error until the next day. But the cheesecake was the best I ever tasted. It was heavy, just the way I like it! The absence of the sour cream (which also saved many calories and much fat) gave it extra "weight."

Here's the recipe for what I call Great Heavy Cheesecake. It's identical to the one on the back of the box, except it doesn't call for a cup of sour cream and I've increased the amount of vanilla extract by fifty per cent (following one of my "Points" at the end of the spice chapter). Here's what you do:

In a bowl, with mixer on high, beat twenty-four ounces of softened (!) cream cheese together with one cup of sugar and three teaspoons of vanilla extract. Beat in three eggs, one at a time. Then pour mixture into the pan.

Bake at three hundred and fifty degrees for sixty to seventy minutes. Then turn off the oven, and with its door slightly ajar, allow the cheesecake to rest in the oven for an hour. Then remove it and let it cool completely (I let it sit at room temperature for an hour). Then pop it into a refrigerator, for at least four hours (but overnight is fine). This is terrific cheesecake!

Be aware of a few things. My cheesecake cracked a little. Linda said perhaps this was more likely because it was heavy. I don't know if this is true, but what's a crack if the cheesecake tastes divine? And if you put on cherry or other toppings, the cracks will be hidden, anyway. Remember, this is a HEAVY cheesecake. If you prefer soft and smooth, add in the cup of sour cream that the box recipe requires.

Successes like this gave me confidence, and I actually began to explore recipe books for ideas and challenges. But I had trouble deciding what to make. The recipe books were all filled with so many different choices, and the pictures made everything look so tempting.

Isn't it incredible what proper lighting and presentation skills can accomplish? The enticing chicken breast is probably filled with more silicon than a Vegas chorus line. And the accompanying asparagus probably spent most of the afternoon with an air brush artist.

My worst photo "duping" occurred when I saw a picture of some puffy orange omelettes. These looked marvelous, proudly strutting skyward out of small souffle cups. The beautiful browning of the omelette tops would have brought tears to even the most heartless chef. I bit.

I separated five eggs (I am proud to say I did this perfectly, and wasn't even nervous doing the fifth!) I added sugar to the whites, flour and orange peel to the yolks, and let both sit overnight in the refrigerator.

The next morning I beat the egg white mixture, and folded it into the yolks. Then I made a sauce, combining orange juice, butter, and brown sugar. Finally, I put some of the sauce in each souffle dish, filled it to the top with the egg mixture, and baked it about fifteen minutes. I then poured the reserved sauce on top.

The good news is that the little omelettes looked outstanding. But when Linda came over for breakfast, we both agreed they tasted like a cross between orange wallpaper paste and silly putty. We would have greatly preferred ordinary omelettes, and they would have been far less work.

In fact, sometimes the recipes that require the least effort wind up being the most tasty. My friend Gail in Chicago gave me a wonderful recipe for a fantastic, easy dessert. I call it Gail's Yogurt-Whipped Topping Delight, and here's what you do:

Allow an eight ounce container of whipped topping to sit out a few minutes at room temperature. Reserve a small amount of it. In a bowl combine the remaining topping with two small containers of yogurt. I love the Yoplait key lime, but use what you wish. You may care to add food coloring, to make the mixture look like the flavor of the yogurt. Then put the mixture in a graham cracker crust (don't tell Gail, she prefers cookie dough).

Cover with the reserved whipped topping, and place in the freezer. About thirty minutes before serving, remove from the freezer and let sit at room temperature.

Gail's dessert sounds so simple you might un-underestimate it. It's FANTASTIC. By the way, I always use low fat yogurt and low fat whipped topping, and to my taste, the dessert doesn't suffer for the substitutions. This recipe is a keeper!

And here's another deceptively easy recipe, for Doris' Incredible Chocolate Fruit Tarts. Everyone will LOVE these. Go to Sam's Club, and in the food aisles find the box with thirty-six small chocolate dessert cups (I'm sure these are sold elsewhere, I've just never seen them). These cups are delicious in and of themselves (they're dark chocolate), and are packaged very well so breakage is not a concern.

Then you just spend a few moments creating a world class filling to put in the cups. With a mixer combine eight ounces of softened cream cheese with eight ounces of powdered sugar. Then use the mixer to whip up eight ounces of heavy cream to fairly stiff peaks, and fold into the cream cheese-powdered sugar mixture. Fill each chocolate cup to the top with this great white stuff (the portions given above make enough for about ten tarts), and decorate the top of each cup with colorful fruits and berries. Your guests will be floored, and will think you paid a caterer five dollars apiece for these beautiful creations!

Although I love experimenting with new recipes, I was saddened by one discovery. Preparing a special meal at home often costs more than eating out. And you have the cleanup to boot!

Once I needed to saute a shrimp appetizer in licorice-flavored spirits. I merely needed two tablespoons, but the smallest bottle at the liquor store set me back fifteen bucks. And the dish was disappointing.

The same thing occurred with a more plebeian concoction, rice pudding. I bought a gallon of milk, although I needed just a cup. Paid over two bucks for a small package of arborio rice that I used a third of. And spent $4.99 on a large bottle of maple syrup, since I assumed the pudding would be delicious and I would remake it. Add in the other ingredients, and I had twelve dollars invested in this simple dessert. It, too, disappointed; I'd have been better off bringing in five servings from Manny's Gyros.

Here is a can't miss idea for some entrepreneur. The day recipes are published in the local newspaper, obtain early copies. Then go to various markets, and assemble individual packages that have all the ingredients for each recipe. For example, one rib of celery, five cherry tomatoes, twelve kalamata olives, one tablespoon of Marsala wine, one lotus root, three scallions, four ounces of chicken broth, eight ounces of apricot nectar.

Keep these in a cooler, stand outside a busy market, and put up a sign. It's my bet recipe lovers will stand in line to throw their money at you!

FREDDY'S TOP EIGHT RECIPE POINTS

- The recipe will usually call for the one kind of vinegar you are out of.

- Buyers of cookbooks are both well read and well fed.

- As long as the dog eats it, a new recipe should be considered a success.

- To find a friend's favorite recipe, find the page in his cookbook with the most stains.

- Throw away every recipe that you haven't made in the last seven years.

- When a friend asks for a recipe, the information you supply should be at least ninety per cent accurate.

- Successfully mastering a dessert recipe is no cake walk.

- When a recipe calls for oil, it doesn't mean Pennzoil.

Toward Competence

Incredibly, I slowly became comfortable in the kitchen! But it was not an easy process. My progress was halting, uneven; for every advance there was equivalent backsliding. I never experienced a mystical, magic moment when everything suddenly became clear.

I merely kept plugging away, and kept an open mind. For me, these were sufficient. I explored new foods, to discover unique tastes and experience the unfamiliar. I utilized my friends as resources, and benefitted greatly by asking them questions and seeing them operate in the kitchen. And I even enrolled in cooking classes, to allow professionals to sharpen my skills further.

I loved tasting new foods, especially at my local

natural foods store. I deliberately sampled a new item every visit. This approach taught me that the world isn't quite yet ready for jicama slaw, and that tofu burgers are no immediate threat to McDonalds.

One day Kung Pao Chicken got my attention. Did it ever! I bought a portion, and took it to the small nearby dining area. With the first bite, I realized that the cayenne peppers and chili peppers were absolutely overwhelming. Perhaps stupidly, I hadn't realized this was a spicy dish, and hadn't bought anything to drink. My mouth was on fire.

Frantically, I approached the cashier and begged for directions to the bottled water section. I raced there, and grabbed the first bottle in sight. I ripped off the cap, and downed the entire container on the spot. It brought relief, as did the comment from a gentleman next to me in the aisle. Said he, eyebrows raised, "That must be tasty water!"

I loved roaming the bulk bin aisles, time very well spent. I discovered roasted soybeans, the easiest and most painless way I know of daily getting soy into your diet. And I was astonished at how much less bulk spices cost than grocery store spices.

I experimented with all kinds of new foods at home, too. Phyllo dough was a blast. Phyllo dough is an extremely thin dough, used in Greek and other ethnic dishes, that you layer, to produce a flaky

UNSAFE ON ANY BURNER

pastry. By the way, most people mispronounce the term. It's FEE-LO-DOH.

I used phyllo one time to make a quirky, fun dish: a Spam Croustade. A croustade is a crisp shell, like a puff pastry, that food is served in. Very fancy, very classic. Spam? Well, you know Spam. It's a little less classic. I became aware of this recipe because it won first prize in the Spam recipe competition at the Wisconsin State Fair. I wanted to work with phyllo dough, so I gave it a try. The Spam Croustade was delicious. If you can't get beyond the Spam, substitute a different meat, or prepare it vegetarian.

Here's what to do: In the frozen food section at your grocer, buy phyllo dough. Allow it to defrost in the fridge for seven hours before use.

First the filling. In a skillet brown one can of diced low sodium Spam, and one-quarter cup onion, in three tablespoons of butter. Cook until tender. Stir in three tablespoons flour, one-quarter teaspoon dried savory (skip it if you're out), and one-quarter teaspoon pepper. Stir and cook one minute. Stir half of this mixture into a bowl with two beaten eggs. Then add the remaining half of the mixture. Fold in five ounces of cooked and well drained frozen spinach, one cup of small curd cottage cheese, and one-half cup crumbled feta cheese. Set aside.

Now the fun part, the phyllo. First, melt a stick

of butter. Then remove the phyllo sheets from the box and stretch them out to full size (they come folded). Working very, very quickly, brush butter along the outside of one phyllo sheet. Then fold it from top to bottom, and then from top to bottom again. Place one end of this sheet in the center of a twelve inch pizza pan, with the other end extending over the side. Keep brushing and folding new phyllo sheets, putting each one in the pizza pan, always slightly overlapping the prior sheet. Once the pizza pan is covered with phyllo (twelve to fourteen sheets), spread the filling in the center of the pan to cover an eight inch diameter circle. Starting with the phyllo sheet you placed down last, and working backwards to the first, lift the far end of each sheet to the center of the pizza pan. Slightly fold back phyllo sheet when it gets there. Drizzle on any remaining butter, and cook thirty to forty minutes in a preheated, three hundred and seventy five degree oven.

Please work rapidly with phyllo; it dries out quickly. Use a damp towel to cover unused sheets. Consider making this with a partner. One individual can butter and fold the phyllo, the other can place it on the pizza pan. Don't be concerned if your folded phyllo sheet tears a little. Just place in on the pizza pan so that the torn part will be on the bottom, and no one will be the wiser.

UNSAFE ON ANY BURNER

I did have one near phyllo disaster which you should know about. The sheets I bought came wrapped in a single, white sheet of paper. My friend Linda mistook it for a phyllo sheet, and was all set to put some butter on its outside edges when I intervened. This isn't as extraordinary a miscue as you might think. The phyllo sheets are sort of opaque, too, and are, after all, paper thin.

My coconut adventures practically matched the excitement of my phyllo. I decided I wanted to taste coconut milk, so for the first time I bought a coconut at the grocer. I was advised that to get to the milk inside, I would need to poke out two of the coconut's eyes. But the shell is very hard; even with a screwdriver I was unsuccessful. While my son laughed, I got out my power drill, and drilled the eyes out. Can't say the milk tasted any good. Then again, I suppose the sawdust didn't help.

As I continued my explorations, probably my best sources of information were my friends. I was so lucky to have them. They were so kind to patiently share their knowledge, regardless of the hour, even though preparing food from scratch often no longer interested them.

Incredibly, they usually managed to keep a straight face, despite my misadventures. Once I was making muffins for a party while my friend Jessica and her two daughters watched. Grabbing the large, unopened box of yellow corn meal, I tried to rip off the top. No success. I sensed that the women were amused. I then used greater force, and created a gigantic tear across the entire top of the box. When I tried to pour, corn meal fell all over the floor and counter. The women remained silent, looking as though they were about to burst. Then one asked, "Did you happen to see the easy opening pour spout on the side?"

Time after time, friends showed me the right way. When honey wouldn't easily pour out of a measuring spoon, Linda advised me to first coat the spoon with oil. Jessica taught me to always measure solids before liquids. That way, solids like rice and sugar don't stick to the measuring cup. Barb instructed me never to leave a sharp knife in the sink, as you can cut yourself when stuffing the garbage disposal. Henry told me to close my kitchen cabinets as soon as possible to avoid head injuries. And Mary advised me to never leave a stirring spoon in a working pot, as it, too, will get hot.

If I was alone when a question arose, I had the luxury of calling a number of friends for help. "How long do I cook asparagus?" "At what temperature do I bake squash?"

This system got its roughest test one Thanksgiving, as I was attempting to stuff a bird for the first time. Initially I called Cindy to verify how many

UNSAFE ON ANY BURNER

things I should remove from the turkey before starting, and where those items were located. Then I dialed Rose for the specifics of her "to die for" stuffing recipe.

Turkey anatomy was new to me. When I innocently asked Rose where to insert the stuffing, she told me. "Come on," I said, sure she was pulling my drumstick. "Where does it really go?" She repeated the destination. "Get serious," I rejoined. "I know I'm a rookie, but don't make a fool of me. Where do I really put the stuffing?"

When she held to her story, I claimed I had to watch a boiling pot, hung up, and speed dialed Cindy. "You'll never guess where Rose said I put the stuffing!" I said. To my amazement, Cindy confirmed Rose's instructions. In the face of such consensus, my familiarity with the details of turkey anatomy expanded enormously.

Despite such willing assistance from those around me, it was clear that I still lacked much information and many skills. My friends were all happy to help me out, but they had lives, too. I couldn't call them every day with my simple questions. After all, making Freddy competent in the kitchen was my goal, not theirs.

For my formal education I went to Homemakers' School. This is a three hour evening program, underwritten by national food companies. A skilled demonstrator prepares fifteen recipes, which are given away as door prizes at the end of the evening. A local food store helps sponsor the event, and makes available a wide assortment of additional door prizes.

I was a tad self-conscious as female after female joined me in the auditorium. Of about three hundred people just twelve were males, and most of them were escorted by a female. Perhaps because I stood out, a reporter from the local community paper snapped my picture. I kept wondering what the guys in the locker room would say, but the picture never ran.

This was just the first of my educational endeavors. A local community college offered a six-session hands-on introduction to cooking, and I enrolled. What a kick! There were about twenty students in the class each Thursday evening, and we broke up into five different groups, each with our very own kitchen area.

I happened to be teamed with Richard the Fat Lover. He'd show up at every session munching a Snickers bar. Whereas other groups chose that evening's recipe based upon ease of preparation or familiarity, Richard had different criteria. He chose the one with the most grams of fat.

Each week, Richard would appall me more than the previous one. If a recipe called for two table-

UNSAFE ON ANY BURNER

spoons of butter, he'd add half a stick. He'd substitute mayonnaise for Miracle Whip. And he even refused to drain the fat from ground beef we'd fried. "That's where all the flavor is," he'd whine. Despite my protests, he'd insist on doing it his way. And if I protested too much, he threatened to call over the instructor. Turned out to actually be a plus. I got into the habit of eating fat free breakfasts and lunches every Thursday!

I'm pleased to say my interactions with other students went far more smoothly. Often we'd help different groups find ingredients in the common storeroom, or answer questions for each other if the teacher was occupied elsewhere. In the process I learned to be more sensitive. Gentlemen, I have some advice for you: don't go up to a group of women folding custard into pastry shells and ask, "How are the tarts?"

Despite this minor (!) faux pas, this class was a great experience. I picked up some good recipes, and benefitted from seeing others perform in the kitchen. I discovered I do one thing that is apparently absurd. When I cut up meat in preparation for cooking, I use a fork and knife. I can't imagine doing it any other way. But apparently almost the whole world uses a knife and their fingers, and thinks me strange.

Having observed fellow rookies in action, I decided to see how the masters operate. The local PBS affiliate held a fundraiser at Milwaukee's wonderful French restaurant, Grenadier's. Since the meal cost eighty dollars per person, the expense was not trivial. Frankly I seldom attend benefits. But the promise of Grenadier's wonderful food and well-deserved reputation for immaculate presentation proved irresistible.

The meal was gorgeous, a term I'd previously reserved for women. It consisted of a terrine of porcinis and chicken with morel sauce, sesame-seared yellow-fin tuna, fresh country greens with a cherry-walnut vinaigrette and a goat cheese crouton, roasted beef tenderloin "Provencale," assorted cheeses, and a flourless chocolate cake with Sauce Anglaise.

What a night! I hadn't realized food could be so pretty and tasty! I even managed to use the proper utensil most of the time, and didn't embarrass Linda at all. I left with a heightened commitment to culinary excellence.

But soon I had a new problem: I was out of control. Unlike my initial rookie days, when I HAD to buy kitchenware, now I WANTED to. I purchased a wonderful set of milkshake glasses, which make plain old ice cream and milk so much fun. And I bought some very nice beer glasses. Just the sight of them forces me to relax, even on evenings I might otherwise be tense.

When loved ones asked me what I wanted for my birthday, or a holiday, "Kitchenware" was my standard reply. For one birthday Bob gave me a mini-chopper; for another, Mike presented me with a nice bottle for salad dressing. Other friends got me serving dishes and souffle dishes.

I bought a book on garnishing fruits and vegetables, and invested in the different implements to make it happen. The first results, though, were not encouraging. Friends thought my carefully crafted lemon pig looked like a pregnant elephant. But I've learned how to form lemon peel into a cute little tail for a lemon, and how to sculpt a lemon so that lemon sorbet can be served from it for dessert.

Here's what you do: Lay a lemon on the counter. With a knife descending from above, cut an oval pattern around the "top." If the lemon is two inches thick, try to cut into it about one and three quarter inches. When you are done cutting the oval, lift off the top. Most of the insides of the lemon will be attached to it. Use your knife to cut the pith from the top. Use a spoon to scoop out any pith remaining in the lemon bottom. Add lemon sorbet to the bottom, cover with the top, and place in freezer for later serving.

As my kitchen became littered with arcane appliances and questionable gadgets, my friends became concerned. "You only have so many cabinets," Linda reminded me. "Rome wasn't built in a day," Jessica assured.

My low point occurred one day when I received my Walter Drake catalogue. Previously I would usually order a poster, or a bumper sticker, and not even notice kitchen gadgets. But this time I flipped out, and felt a need to shop compulsively. I covered a blank sheet of paper, as well as the enclosed order form, with my purchases. By the time I called Jessica to share my enthusiasm, I was suffering from writer's cramp.

"You're ordering a WHAT?" she asked. "Two large pans," I replied, "so that I can make edible baskets from baked flour tortillas." "People aren't into baskets any more," she said. "They want wraps. And what good are two? Won't you be having four for dinner?" But then she hit me with the zinger. "By the way, aren't you the one who doesn't particularly like Mexican food, and tries to avoid ground beef, cheese, and sour cream?" I agreed she had a point. Truthfully, lots of points. I crossed the items off my list.

But then I excitedly told her about my skim ladle, an engineer's dream! The handle included a trigger, and by depressing it, fat would miraculously ascend through the straw-like attachment from the soup or gravy to the attached containment bowl.

UNSAFE ON ANY BURNER

"How can I resist?" I said.

"But will you use it?" she asked. "Of course I will," I responded. "You know I make lots of soups." She was ready with an answer. "But you make chicken soup. That isn't all that fatty. And you rarely make gravies." She had a point, so I deleted it also.

Item after item fell victim to Jessica's common sense ax. I tossed away the additional sheet of paper, and condensed my ever-shrinking list on a small section of the standard order form. By the time we hung up, all that remained was a bumper sticker, and my lemon zester. What is life without a lemon zester?

As a result of all these experiences, whether it be trying new foods, seeking advice from friends, attending classes, or buying unique housewares, I reached a point where I actually, finally UNDERSTOOD what cooking was about. I had enough confidence in my abilities to make decisions myself.

The first time this occurred was a pleasant surprise; I was preparing Thanksgiving turkey stuffing, and was following the recipe on the bag (Rose's stuffing had really not been so great the prior year). I combined the bread cubes with water, and was sauteing some celery, mushrooms, and onions. But the recipe indicated I should add an entire stick of

.124

.124

.124

butter to the bread cube/water combo. In my literal rookie days, I'd have done so. But now I instinctively knew that the little butter from the saute pan would be more than sufficient.

Shortly thereafter I made another intelligent decision, about new measuring cups and spoons. I was in a department store, and a sales associate showed me a very cheap set. It was a "combo," with measuring cup on one end of the handle and the measuring spoon on the other. "How handy," I thought. "They're far less expensive than buying separate spoons and cups."

I was about to buy them. But then I remembered all the times my measuring cups lay buried in a disgusting sink while I still needed a measuring spoon. I certainly wouldn't want to fish one out.

With great satisfaction I looked at the salesperson and said, "Sorry, these aren't for me." I then proudly headed for the escalator, to begin my ascent to even further culinary heights.

FREDDY'S TOP EIGHT
COMPETENCE POINTS

- If two women give you conflicting advice, follow that of the woman you're dating.

- No one really needs a left handed double boiler.

- Don't let phyllo dough be Greek to you.

- Always know the location of the bottled water aisle when you sample new foods in a natural foods store.

- Selecting the perfect cheese is no feta compli.

- Women can generally fit twice as much into a dishwasher as a man.

- Individuals who love kitchen gadgets should marry cabinet makers.

- A chef who doesn't turn out pretty food should have his wages garnished.

Wok on the Wild Side

As I became more and more comfortable with American cuisine, my interests drifted to the exotic. And Asia was my first stop.

Wanting to learn more about foods of the region, I visited a local Asian market. What a great place. The owner is so patient with my questions, and seeing so many unfamiliar products is a thrill. I'd never seen three-quarters of the vegetables, and in the cooler I confronted a new concept: quality mystery meat.

What's also thrilling is that prices in ethnic markets are far lower than in the big grocery stores. One would assume just the opposite, that the mass merchants would dramatically underprice the mom and pop, single-store entrepreneur. But it's not so. Coconut milk costs about fifty per cent less at the Asian store, as do the specialty noodles. So when you visit, you get adventure AND savings.

You may recall that I purchased a wok at a rummage sale when I was setting up my kitchen. So from day one I'd done lots of stir frys. Practically lived on them. Using the traditional Chinese stir fry recipe—three tablespoons soy sauce, three tablespoons dry sherry, and one tablespoon of corn starch—I'd let my meat (usually diced chicken) marinate for twenty minutes in the fridge, and then cook the meat and marinade in the wok. When it was done, I'd take it out and saute onions. Once they were translucent (about four minutes), I'd add the chicken back in along with sliced tomatoes, and cook for about two minutes. Stir Fry Heaven is terrific over a bed of rice.

But I wanted to do more than stir fry. Serendipity struck! Mary, my neighbor, had a friend who volunteered to teach me how to make egg rolls, and I jumped at the chance. But a crisis developed. You see, I had an accident. As I was turning one of the frying egg rolls, I dropped it (I was using chopsticks). As I had lifted the egg roll fairly high, it splattered a fair amount of oil when it fell back into the pan, directly on Linda's and my fingers.

This inaugurated every woman's favorite game, claiming the man's a baby when he's in pain. My finger really hurt me. It was burned. I soaked the finger in a glass of coldish water, but when I would remove it, the heat still in my finger would cause hurt, and I'd need to return it to the glass. Linda, meanwhile, looked at me skeptically, and told me her burn was far worse.

Our phone lines crackled all the next day, as we exchanged charges and countercharges. I said her pain couldn't be greater, as she hadn't needed to soak her finger. She said I was a big baby. As we broached the limits of our skills for sarcasm, clearly it was time for action: a wager. As ridiculous as it sounds, we made a bet to see whose blister would be worse in two days. I gazed at my welt repeatedly during this time period, checking its appearance, not sure whether I wanted it to go away or not. For a pathetic, desperate second I thought of trying to make it worse.

On the big day I arrived at Linda's house brimming with confidence. She showed me her welt; it was about four times what mine was. I forked over my three bucks, departed as quickly as my seriously deflated ego would permit, and swore to wear gloves the next time I attempted to master Chinese specialty dishes.

Happily, my exploration of Chinese cooking unexpectedly resolved a longtime family mystery. My son Mike has always loved a particular Chinese

UNSAFE ON ANY BURNER

restaurant in Milwaukee. It's not that he adores the egg roll, or the mu shu pork. What he loves is more basic. He loves the rice. And he loves it because, as he says, it's "sticky."

Whenever we eat at the restaurant, we ask the management how the rice is prepared. And their answer is always the same, "Put the rice in water and boil." Each time I make rice for Mike I alter the proportions, hoping to replicate the desired, "sticky" effect. Each time I fail. I look at him hopefully as the fork enters his mouth, but always I hear those two deflating words, "Not sticky."

Then one evening I was at a friend's house, and she was preparing a Chinese stir fry. "Would you like it over sticky rice?" she asked. "Pardon me," I said, in disbelief. "Sticky rice," she said. "Would you like your stir fry over sticky rice?" "Over what?" I asked. "Sticky rice," she repeated. "S-T-I-C-K-Y R-I-C-E. Sticky rice. Are you hard of hearing?"

I told her about my family mystery, and she went on to tell me about sticky rice. It's a special kind, that sticks. You just need to know enough to ask for it at the Asian store. She was nice enough to let me have some, and as soon as I returned home I called Mike to invite him over for a stir fry the following evening.

I was full of excitement as I filled the saucepan

with water and the special rice. I measured each ingredient with extra precision. I closely monitored heat during the cooking process. Twenty minutes later, when I called Mike to the table, my heart was beating as fast as it could.

Mike took one bite and snapped to attention. He smiled, and chewed with an air of disbelief. Then he turned to me, and with a smile etched across his face, uttered the one word I'd been waiting so long to hear: "Sticky!"

Proud of my accomplishments in Chinese cooking, I explored other Asian cuisines. Several excellent local restaurants sparked my interest in Thai. I just love the flavors, so I've dined in quite a few Thai restaurants at this point.

Initially I prepared Thai dishes at home that I'd loved in restaurants, but have since moved on to tackling recipes at will. Here are my two favorite.

The first is Chicken Soup with Shrimp, Scallions, and Lemongrass. Lemongrass is a ubiquitous Thai ingredient. Fresh lemongrass comes in a stalk, and looks a little bit like celery. It's not spicy but is very flavorful, and it gives most Thai soups their distinctive taste. It comes dried, and can be bought in spice houses, but fresh is best.

Here's what you do to the lemongrass. Tear off the outer layers, trim off the hard ends, and cut what remains into three-inch pieces. If you care to,

you can take hold of some of the pieces and partially tear them along their middle (lengthwise),
so even more flavor escapes.

After your chicken broth has boiled, turn the heat
down, and put in four to six pieces of lemongrass.
Let the pot sit for four to five minutes. Then remove the inedible lemongrass (with a slotted spoon
if possible), bring the soup once again to boil, and
add the diced scallions and uncooked shrimp.
When the shrimp are pink (usually a minute or
two), soup's on. It's a real treat.

By the way, at the Asian market you might want
to buy a can of straw mushrooms. These are the
Chinese-style mushrooms often found in chow
mein, etc. Add them in with the shrimp, and you'll
have additional fun and flavor.

When making this soup, please try to avoid my
rookie mistake. The first time I made it, guests were
due any minute. Everything was running on schedule. But when I had to remove the lemongrass from
the pot, my timetable disintegrated.

I brought forth my colander from the cabinet, and
confidently positioned it squarely in the middle of
my sink. I reached for the potholders, and carefully
carried the hot soup pot over to the colander.

Just then, there was a knock on the door, and I
put down the pot and welcomed my first guest,
Jessica. She joined me in the kitchen. As I again

raised the pot over the colander, the smile disappeared from Jessica's face, as she sensed imminent disaster. I skillfully poured the soup into the colander, holding firmly to the hot pot so it wouldn't fall and send my delicious broth slithering across my kitchen floor. But can you see anything wrong with this picture? Jessica did, but she couldn't sound her warning in time. I neglected to have a bowl under the colander; poured all my delicious broth down the drain!

Another great Thai dish is Curried Chicken with Coconut Milk and Avocados. This is so easy it is ridiculous. And it's wonderful.

Here's what to do. In a wok or frying pan, place a tablespoon or two of oil. Then add a can of Masaman Curry Paste, which is real easy to find at an Asian market (it's about the size of a can of tuna). Combine the curry paste with about four tablespoons of coconut milk, and stir until paste is well blended. Then add what remains from the opened can of coconut milk, as well as one other entire can. Bring to boil. Add one-half cup of chicken stock, and one-third of a cup of brown sugar. Let boil for a minute, and then reduce heat to create a gentle boil. Let mixture cook thirty minutes, stirring occasionally.

When approximately thirty minutes has elapsed, add diced chicken to the wok or fry pan. Bring back to full boil and then reduce heat to medium, cooking chicken for two minutes. At that point turn off the heat, and let chicken remain in the hot coconut milk for approximately four more minutes. Place the curried chicken on a bed of rice, garnish with avocado slices to cut the spice, and you'll be in heaven.

And that's it. Do you see how simple this is? Other than slicing the chicken, there's no work at all. The curry and the coconut create a tasty, unique flavor combination. Everyone will love this. And it's perfect for a party. You can be with your guests, not with your food.

By the way, there are a few things you should know about coconut milk. It is loaded with fat. That's why I use the low-fat variety. Perhaps I give up a little taste, but it's a tradeoff I can live with.

Be aware that sometimes coconut milk in the can is liquid, while at other times it is solid. The first time I came across solid coconut milk I feared it might be spoiled. I've since learned this is nothing per se to be worried about; it's apparently the fat that solidifies. The milk quickly turns into a liquid once it is heated.

In addition to Chinese and Thai, I also experimented with Japanese cuisine. I was visiting my friends Gail and Ronnie in Chicago. Gail was preparing sushi for a party that night. So I tasted it,

FRED GOSMAN

became intrigued, and watched Gail closely as she prepared that evening's appetizer.

One thing that surprised me is that raw fish is not a requirement for sushi. It's an optional ingredient. You can prepare sushi with rice and vegetables, or whatever you wish.

If I can make sushi, anyone can. It's easy! Here's what you do. Go to an Asian market and buy seaweed paper (perhaps your grocer might have it, too). This is called "nori" in Japanese. In each package there will be about ten six-inch-by-eight-inch sheets.

Take the first sheet, and place it on your counter with the shiny side down and the widest side of the sheet parallel to the counter edge. Spread cooked sticky rice all over the sheet. Then add the ingredients you prefer. Gail used thin julienne strips of cucumber and avocado, and these worked great. Here's how you do it:

At the bottom of the sheet of seaweed paper, place next to each other, across the entire width of the paper, one thin row of cucumber and one thin row of avocado (each cut lengthwise). Then grate carrot thinly over the entire piece of seaweed paper. Starting at the bottom, fold the seaweed paper over the strips of cuke and avocado, and keep rolling to the top, when you'll have a tube. Then, using a sharp knife, slice the tube into smaller pieces. Each tube will make about six pieces.

Then all you have to do is dip the sushi in sauce. Soy sauce works well, and it's easy to buy. There are two other traditional condiments, tougher to find outside of an Asian market, that often are added to the soy sauce: wasabi paste and pickled ginger. Making sushi was a great experience. It was lots of fun, and it was very satisfying introducing my guests to such a unique dish.

Whether I was making Chinese, Thai, or Japanese, I loved the fact that I welcomed new ideas, and was willing to take risks. But sometimes I took things for granted, with disastrous consequences.

I invited two Asian friends over for dinner, and made a great spicy spare rib recipe I'd discovered. They absolutely adored it. But I made a teenie-weenie blunder. I focused so much on buying quality spare ribs that I forgot about the rice. And when I went to prepare the meal, the only kind I had was Minute Rice.

It takes a certain amount of courage to serve Minute Rice to Asians. I tried to hide the fact, forbidding them from entering my kitchen. And I attempted to exude a boyish, confident strut as I brought the rice to the table.

But these ladies knew their rice. "What kind of rice is this?" one asked, an instant after her first bite. She appeared upset, but perhaps this was my

FRED GOSMAN

imagination. "I'm not sure," I replied. "I experiment with different varieties all the time."

Then my other guest entered into the conversation. "It's really quite different. Unique. Did you do anything unusual to it?" "No," I responded. "How are the ribs?" I asked, trying to detract attention from my questionable starch.

But they persisted. Finally they asked, "You're not serving us Uncle Ben's, are you?" Calling forth all my courage, I decided to fess up. Told them it was Minute Rice. And they were great sports.

Troubling as this experience was, I benefitted from it. You see Mary, my neighbor, had her father visiting from Italy. I wanted to meet the gentleman, so I was expecting Mary and her dad for dinner the following evening. I was planning on spaghetti. After twenty minutes of reflection, I decided to reconsider the Chef Boyardee.

FREDDY'S TOP EIGHT
ASIAN CUISINE POINTS

- The key to Chinese cooking is to apply spices ginger-ly.

- A person who orders his meal "hot" in a Thai restaurant has a stomach made of steel.

- Visiting an ethnic market shouldn't be a foreign experience.

- A man who makes Minute Rice for Asians will have guests who are boiling mad.

- Making sushi doesn't have to be a fishy experience.

- People who consume great quantities of coconut milk are living off the fat of the land.

- Burns suffered while cooking will always hurt a man more than they will hurt a woman.

- If I can successfully experiment with Asian cuisine, anyone can.

Dinner Is Served

Incredibly enough, over time I turned into a comfortable host. The guy who used to panic if a friend stopped by for chips and salsa was now capable of feeding twelve without losing sleep or guests.

Of course I was terribly nervous during my initial parties, mentally contemplating a slew of likely disasters. What if I forget a course? What if the dessert doesn't turn out? What if my guests hate the wine? Expecting the worst, I usually wasn't disappointed.

Then I discovered that planning made most of my tension disappear. The more on top of things I was, the less nervous I felt. I tried to shop ahead of time so all the food was in place. I made a meticulous list of everything needed, leaving nothing to chance.

The evening of the dinner, I used a timeline to remind myself when to complete specific, required tasks. Put in the potatoes at 6:45. Remove the dessert from the fridge to thaw at 8:00. Everything and anything made my list. This might seem overly structured, but once I knew everything was written down, I was more relaxed and felt more in control.

I began to work smarter, too. As I did my pre-party prep, I'd wash the dishes as they became dirty; I didn't want to confront a mess later. I cleaned up my work areas as I went along, putting away the can opener the instant I was through with it, or discarding empty cans at once. And I'd always do the dishes that evening, before retiring; the thought of facing dishes in the morning took some of the joy out of the occasion.

So I could relax and enjoy my guests, I tried to have most of the work done by the time they arrived. Soups and salads were made ahead of time. I selected entrees that either cooked quickly, so my absence from my guests wasn't lengthy, or entrees that cooked slowly, and needed little ongoing attention. I even had water in the coffee maker, and coffee in the filter. All I had to do to make some java after dinner was touch the "on" switch.

If I made a mistake, I learned from it. The first time I had eight guests, I received quite an education. The timing of my soup was off; I neglected to account for the fact the greater the liquid, the longer the cooking time. And I ran out of plates and utensils.

As I began to enjoy entertaining, I knew I wanted to upgrade my dining room table. Initially all I had was a card table. When I read in the classifieds about an oak table with six chairs and tablepads for $275, I was intrigued. I bought it the instant I saw it.

What a difference! It absolutely MADE my living room. I was so happy to have it. But a table won't do anything for your dinner party if it's not appropriately decked out.

So I got into place mats, big time. But I had a problem. I often bought ugly ones. Eventually I wouldn't use my new purchases until a female friend gave me the color go-ahead. Saved me lots of aggravation, and beautified my table, too.

But there's a real issue with place mats. How many to buy? At least four, right; you're going to have guests. But where do you stop? Six place mats? Eight? Twelve? The same issue applies to cloth napkins. I never truly discovered the "magic" place mat number, but now just buy four or six cloth napkins, and alternate them around the table with

UNSAFE ON ANY BURNER

another, coordinating set at my larger dinner parties.

I began to take great pride in setting a pretty table. The first sign of my emerging "table presence" was napkin rings. The concept really tickled me. I have six different sets, although I usually use the basic white ones. These aren't expensive at all, and provide a luxurious touch to the table.

I also became a candle lover! Light them all the time, even with my boys, even when I'm alone. Mike gave me a butane lighter for ease in lighting. Candles provide a great sense of peace and hope. Buy them, light them, enjoy them—they're one of the nicest mini-luxuries around.

Lovely floral centerpieces also graced my table, although I learned the hard way not to let my interest get out of proportion. Once I bought a lovely bouquet at my grocer, a lovely LARGE bouquet. I took such pride in arranging it in my vase. It dominated the center of the table, providing a beautiful setting for a delicious meal.

But there was a problem. None of us could see the person directly across the table; the arrangement blocked the view. Each person had to move his head to the right or left to make eye contact with the person opposite. And if both people moved the same direction, the flowers were still in the way!

A beautiful wine carafe graced my table, too. This is a must, especially if you need to hide the vintage. I'm no expert on wine, and frankly can't tell cheaper from better. In fact, Gail and Ronnie in Chicago specifically request "cheap" merlot; they like it best. Do I know how to pick friends, or what?

By the way, I started a nice tradition you might want to consider. A cork collection. Every time I open a bottle of wine, I throw the cork into a big bowl. Corks all are different in appearance, and have the name of the wine imprinted on them. As my bowl fills up, it's a wonderful remembrance of relaxed, happy times.

Surprisingly, the dietary restrictions of my guests rarely came up as an issue. Rather extraordinary, really, given how many people are eating low fat, or vegetarian.

However, there was an incident with Paula's husband, Keith, that was a little touchy. He and Paula came for dinner, and he hates most vegetables. I was planning an asparagus soup. I had a backup soup for him, black bean, in case he hated the asparagus, but Paula and I thought he'd like the soup if we could hide its name from him (the soup went through the blender, so no asparagus were visible).

As Jessica and I sat in the living room with them before dinner the four of us made pleasant conversation. But then Paula innocently asked, "What kind of soup are we having tonight?" I appeared surprised by the question, and proudly replied, "The French favorite, Rue de Vosstag."

Paula practically jumped out of her seat, so excited was she at the prospect of tasting such "classic" cuisine. "I just love that soup. It's so much work. I'll bet it's eight years since I've had it."

Paula and I could hardly control ourselves as we headed for the table. Jessica knew of the ruse, and all three of us dove right into the soup, waxing poetic about its exquisite, complex taste. Out of the corners of our eyes we breathlessly watched Keith take his first tentative spoonful. He swirled the soup around his mouth for what seemed like an eternity; we rejoiced as we saw the movement of his Adam's apple confirm a swallow.

Jessica, Paula, and I could now relax, and concentrate on our soups. But the three of us lost control a few seconds later, when to our amazement vegetable-hating Keith requested a second bowl of "Rue Whatever."

Of course, if dietary needs change suddenly, all rules are off. George and Linda were coming for dinner, and I knew both loved shrimp. So I was throwing a shrimp extravaganza. Shrimp were in the soup, the salad, and the noodle dish.

Five minutes before my guests were due, the

phone rang. It was Linda. She said they were still planning on showing up, but that George was a little under the weather. "He has gout," she said. I expressed concern, but she assured me it's usually controllable with simple dietary changes. "It's no big deal," Linda said. "The only thing he has to avoid is shellfish."

At the party George ate well, and just avoided the shrimp. The three others at the table tried to act saddened by his illness. But our empathy would have been more credible if we hadn't spent so much time fighting over his shrimp.

Even serving someone's favorite food doesn't assure that a party will come off without a hitch. One time the wife of a friend was out of town, so I invited him and his daughter over for dinner. I asked him what his daughter liked, and he indicated she adored chicken.

Well, the chicken was in the oven, and my guests were due in fifteen minutes. The flowers were on the table, the flatwear glistened. All was perfect. As they'd never been to my apartment, I left the door partially ajar to signal which unit was mine.

But then a scary thing happened. The smoke alarm in the hall sounded. This threw me for a jolt; never before had it sounded. Concerned, I raced out of my apartment to investigate. There was no fire; the alarm was activated by smoke from my

UNSAFE ON ANY BURNER

baking chicken, which was escaping through my open door.

But now I had a REAL problem. When I left my apartment, I closed the door behind me. And it locks automatically. And I didn't have my keys with me. Here I was, expecting guests in ten minutes, stranded in the hallway with my oven going. I pounded on six neighbors' doors, and eventually found a phone from which to call my landlord. But he couldn't be there in less than forty-five minutes.

So I took up position in front of my apartment, and waited for my guests. "How nice of you to greet us," my friend said. "Not as nice as you think," I responded. I filled them in, and apologized for needing to wait for the landlord.

He arrived on schedule, and let me in with the pass key. But my chicken was terribly overcooked. I apologized to my friend, and took him and his daughter out to eat. My friend was understanding, but his daughter was ecstatic. Turns out, KFC was her favorite, anyway.

At many of my dinner parties, I WOW my guests with two special dishes, one an appetizer, the other a dessert, which make great presentations. The appetizer is Egg Toppers. Basically, these are scrambled eggs, topped with a touch of sour cream and a snip of chives. What makes this dish so special is that it is served in an egg shell!!

How? First you buy a gadget called an egg topper, available in some kitchenware stores for about six bucks. But be careful. Don't get an egg slicer or an egg poacher. It must be a TOPPER. Call ahead and be specific.

This device neatly slices off part of the shell of a fresh, un-hardboiled egg. Merely insert the egg into the topper as far as it will go. Then simply depress the scissors-like handle, and the topper's teeth will magically do their thing.

After "topping" each shell, pour the egg into a bowl, and refrigerate, for later use. Rinse out the now empty shells with running water. But for extra safety, allow them to lay immersed in a big pot of boiling water for fifteen minutes. Afterwards, place the egg shells upside down in the egg carton, and return it to the fridge.

When you are ready to prepare the dish, take out the carton and turn over the egg shells. Scramble some eggs, and fill each shell almost to the top. Put on a small amount of sour cream (too much makes the eggs cool off too quickly). Then snip on some chives. When finished, close the cover of the egg carton, and carry it to the table. Each of your guests will marvel as you open the carton and display these treasures, and will enthusiastically eat two apiece.

Be aware of a few things. Brown eggs work best;

UNSAFE ON ANY BURNER

they enhance the visual impact. The one time I prepared this with Eggbeaters and fat-free sour cream, the toppers still tasted fine. Also, your guests will appreciate small spoons to make scooping up the egg easier. And you'll need an egg cup for each guest. I have eight glass egg cups, that look like chickens, which cost about $1.75 apiece. But shot glasses work fine, too.

And I made a great discovery. Most of us already have all the egg cups we'll need, whether we know it or not. Simply place a napkin ring on its side, and it becomes a perfect egg cup!

The dessert I astonish my guests with is Raspberry Marvel. It is SO easy. First, preheat the broiler. Then fill small souffle cups, or oven-safe custard cups, with raspberries. Cover the berries with sour cream, and put some brown sugar on top. Place the cups about three inches from the broiler, and broil for three minutes.

These look elegant and taste great. Everyone loves them, and the colors are so pretty. I've found it easiest to remove individual cups from the broiler with a metal spatula. And be aware you'll need about a half-pint (eight ounces) of raspberries for every two servings.

Of all the various dinners I've prepared, I'm proudest of my Thanksgivings. For starters, it's my favorite holiday. I love the sense of family it evokes.

FRED GOSMAN

Even in my early days, when I knew nothing about cooking, I always prepared a festive meal with all the fixings.

The first time I bought a turkey, I was amazed how cheap it was, just thirty-eight cents a pound on special at my grocer. The whole fourteen pound bird cost pennies over five bucks! I predictably went overboard. "At these prices, why not buy more than one?" I said to myself. So I bought three. I was astonished that one turkey buyers couldn't intuitively grasp the wisdom of this approach.

I was quite proud of my coup until I returned home, and discovered there was no room in my freezer for number two and number three. I gave them each to friends, which tripled the effective per-pound cost of turkey number one. By the way, whatever the cost of your bird, protect your investment by remembering that it can take two to three days for a turkey to defrost in the refrigerator.

I cook a delicious turkey every year, and I attribute it to my approach. I treat it like a plant. I talk nice to it. Speak quietly, calmly, and enthusiastically. And baste lovingly, with gentle motions that don't startle.

Actually, I feel sorry for turkeys. Perhaps it's because I'm a middle-aged man, and can empathize with performance anxiety. Think what it must be like for them. They're selected solely on the basis of their physical appearance. During the stuffing process, they're routinely poked and prodded with no concern for their feelings. When baking they confront the rage of the chef if their little thing doesn't pop up exactly on schedule. And after the meal, regardless how good they are, they're remembered as just another piece of meat.

Each year I make my boys turkey, dressing, mashed potatoes, cranberry sauce, pumpkin pie, and sweet potato pie. People love my cranberry sauce; guests always ask for the recipe. I just follow the directions on the package of whole cranberries. I combine the cranberries in a frying pan with water and sugar and heat. That's it. Mash the berries a bit as they get soft, and you have world class cranberry sauce. Try it!

I also make a very good pumpkin pie. I use lots of seasonings, like cinnamon, cloves, ginger, and nutmeg. Don't misinterpret me, I like the taste of pumpkin. But a good pumpkin pie tastes like more than pumpkin. Add the spices; your tummy will thank you.

In addition to making a delicious dinner, I try to make my home look really special for Thanksgiving. I clean it as best I can, and I take out the turkey plates from the cabinets. These are large dinner plates, with a big turkey in the middle, that belonged to my parents. They just loved them; would use them every Thanksgiving. As mom and dad are both deceased, using their plates makes me feel as if they are dining with us.

The first year I hosted Thanksgiving, I started a great tradition I highly recommend. I bought a large "Happy Thanksgiving" poster, and have it in my living room when my guests arrive. I ask each person to write a short note on the back of the poster. Years from now, as I gaze back upon the thoughtful writings of my many guests, this seven dollar poster will be one of my most highly prized possessions.

Unfortunately, last year I went overboard with the Thanksgiving theme, with disastrous consequences. I have a wonderful plant in my living room, a peace lily. It's not outrageously big as these go, but I love it.

Do you recall that when I discovered my fondue fork at the bank, I received several hundred dollars for my change? Well, I was so happy to receive such a windfall, I took twelve of those dollars and celebrated, purchasing for my planter a wooden stick adorned with a gaily decorated, colorful bird's head.

I rushed home with it, and couldn't wait to marry up the stick with my planter. It looked terrific. The turkey head established a perfect tone for the Thanksgiving season.

But then I got thinking. The visual impact of the head was diminished by some taller, nearby leaves, so I cut them back. And then the really dangerous idea occurred to me. Gazing at the plant, with the turkey head on one side, I thought it looked a little bit like a turkey. I therefore decided to shape it into one.

I spent around twenty minutes on the project, variously cutting, and then moving away to consider my handiwork from a distance. When I was done I was ecstatic. Looked just like a turkey. Excited, I called Paula, urging her to come over to see my surprise. I fantasized that my plant might make the cover of a gardening magazine.

When she entered the apartment, she immediately noticed the bird's head. "What a cute toucan," she said. "Pardon me," I replied. "Toucan. Your bird's head. Where'd you get it?" Realizing I was in deep trouble, I didn't even bother to disclose my attempt at turkey topiary.

There was still hope, however; my boys weren't bird experts like Paula. When they arrived for dinner, I allowed them to relax for a few minutes. Then I brought the planter over to them, and asked what they thought of it. Mike said it was "pretty."

"What do you think of the bird's head?" I asked. "It's very nice," Bob said, returning his gaze to the football game on TV.

FRED GOSMAN

I should have quit while I was ahead. But I was so proud of my creation, I just had to ask. "What do you think the plant looks like as a whole?"

Mike was first to answer, and his words should be a warning to all those considering over-decorating for Thanksgiving. With a straight face he looked at me and said, "It looks like a dead toucan. By the way, what time is dinner?"

I took it like a man. I cheered on his football team, tore up my topiary license, and meekly returned to the kitchen for further basting.

FREDDY'S TOP EIGHT DINNER POINTS

- Never put a paper napkin in a wooden napkin ring.

- The cheaper the wine, the lovelier the carafe.

- Guests who show up early for dinner parties should be put to work.

- Be good to your turkey, and it will be good to you.

- Planning an appropriate menu is a matter of good taste.

- Guests who don't leave after your third yawn should be required to do the dishes.

- Never trust a wine not sold by the gallon.

- If the first to finish had to do the dishes, men would eat more slowly.

Sex and the Single Chef

As a single man, I was very interested in finding a woman who shared my interest in cooking. Unfortunately, the task proved more daunting than I expected.

The ladies whom my friends fixed me up with were decidedly anti-cooking. One woman hadn't turned on her stove for a month. Another had a policy of not visiting a grocery store more frequently than every other week. Nor did I encounter greater success with the females I met at work. The lady in the next office asked, "Why do you cook? Haven't you heard of restaurants?" An administrator informed me it's most efficient to leave food preparation to the professionals.

So how could I meet women? I thought and

UNSAFE ON ANY BURNER

thought. I talked about it with friends and I finally decided on a radical course: I would meet them in the grocery store. At least then I would know that they didn't eat EVERY meal out.

The first time I went into action, I was extremely nervous. As luck would have it, every woman who interested me seemed to have on a wedding ring. Over time I relaxed, and am pleased to report my share of both successes and failures.

My first foray was stillborn, waylaid by a deliciously creative excuse. I was in line at my local market, and it was three o'clock in the afternoon on the day before Thanksgiving. The store was mobbed, as I nervously chatted with the woman next to me in our slow-moving line. She was an English teacher, and it seemed like we had a lot in common. With heart racing and throat dry, I invited her to join me for coffee.

"Thank you for the wonderful offer," she said. "But I need to get back to my house. A drywaller is coming over to start some work."

Does this ring true to you? How many drywallers are starting work late in the afternoon on the day before Thanksgiving? Further, deer hunting season started two days previous, a big day in Wisconsin. Most tradesmen are out in the woods. So I wished her luck with her "renovation," and said goodbye.

This was the first of many excuses. Fully four of

the females I approached claimed they were in fact married, that their rings were "coincidentally" at the jeweler being fixed.

Sometimes reality jolted me, too. One Sunday morning I stopped at a busy market to purchase some snack food before a Green Bay Packer game. The place was packed.

I nervously glanced at my watch as I slowly worked my way up to the front of the checkout line. "I hope I get home in time for the kickoff," I said to myself. After what seemed like an eternity, I was next.

But then I saw her, a smashing young lady, just entering the rear of the other express line. She seemed so open, so friendly. And she had a warm, broad smile. This was a defining moment. I had to choose, football or flirtation? Romance won.

I pretended that I forgot to purchase an item, and left my line. I then swiftly joined her at the rear of hers. "What a crazy encounter this will be," I said to myself. I imagined the bizarre circumstances of our meeting would make a great story to share at a potential wedding.

We spoke casually for awhile, and then I introduced myself. She was very pleasant, and seemed to have a great sense of humor. Unfortunately for me, she had been seeing the same man for three years. When I finally got to the front of the line, I paid my bill and walked briskly to my car. I was looking forward to what was left of the football game, and didn't glance back.

Sometimes I connected with people at the supermarket through utter chance. Once some friends set me up with a woman, and we met for coffee. But as there was no chemistry, neither of us followed up. Later that year I was at a grocery store, and approached a woman for help in selecting the right kind of chicken for chicken soup.

"I know you," she said. "We had coffee six months ago." Well, we talked awhile, and she gave me her new phone number. Two weeks later she came over for dinner, chicken awaiting in the pot. Guess what? Still no chemistry.

Another lady attracted me with her chutzpah. Once I was doing a late shopping for a Friday evening dinner party, and I asked a married woman for help in selecting a tomato ready for eating that evening. She took her task most seriously, and after touching half the tomatoes in the bin, pointed to a particularly ripe one.

But then a different lady interjected. "This one looks good, also," she said. She had overheard my request for help, and was just trying to be of service. I admired her risk-taking, and her obvious sense of ease around strangers. So we chatted awhile; unfortunately for me, she was in the midst of a move to Boston.

One time a woman bagged me at the supermarket. I was buying ingredients for a rice pudding recipe, and asked her for aid in finding something. She was quite helpful, and volunteered that she LOVED rice pudding. I showed her the recipe, which I was carrying with me. "I should really let you know how the pudding turns out," I joked. The next thing I knew, she was handing me a slip of paper with her phone number. We went out a few times, but nothing developed.

Given the hit-and-miss success of these experiences, I decided my social life deserved better, and tried a new approach: I ran a personal ad.

But I didn't just run ANY personal ad. I believe I ran history's first personal ad solely devoted to seeking members of the opposite sex who love to cook. Here it is, exactly as it appeared in the Milwaukee Journal Sentinel:

LET'S COOK

Really! DWPM, 50, really into cooking. Seeks WF to share skills and recipes. Call if you've got the thyme. Knowledge of phyllo dough a plus.

Most of my friends couldn't believe I had resorted to such extreme tactics. A casual acquaintance no-

ticed the ad while reading the personals, and unaware she was speaking to its author, joked, "What
nut would place an ad like this?"

As perhaps you know, individuals who place
personal ads also need to record a short message,
so that those who respond have the opportunity to
hear the ad-writer's voice. In my audio segment, I
merely restated what was in the ad, adding the fact
that I make a cauliflower soup "to die for." I waited
impatiently for my ad to hit (you need to submit it
about two weeks before it runs), and hoped for an
overwhelming response.

Twelve (!!!) females elected to pursue the mad
chef, although much to my amazement, many call-
ers expressed anti-cooking sentiments. "I like to
cook, but I much prefer to be cooked for." "I'll make
a meal as long as it's not too difficult." "I can pour
on a can of soup as well as the next person."

After reviewing the responses, I decided to call
five of the women. The first one sounded rather
pleasant, but unfortunately was very recently divorced and wasn't ready to date seriously. On top
of that, she gave the distinct impression that her
hamburger frequently needed to be helped.

Number two lived an hour away. We met halfway for coffee. All I heard were complaints about
the drive, so where was the future? I was disappointed, too, that when she told me which gour-

met items she liked to prepare, meatloaf headed the list.

I was excited by the third woman, who loved to cook. But when we met, there was no chemistry. She did, however, extend me the courtesy of a prized cheesecake recipe.

The fourth woman sounded really pleasant, and in fact she used to teach a cooking class at a local community college. Obviously I had more than met my match. But she re-established ties with a former mate (or so she said), and our date for coffee never came off.

The fifth woman sounded perfect on the phone. She was funny, relaxed, and enjoyed talking about her cooking misadventures as well as successes. I was excited to meet her, but feared there would again be no chemistry.

Boy, was I wrong. Sparks flew. We were terribly compatible. When we eventually cooked together on our second date, not just the stove was turned on. She was a relaxed, wonderful cook, and I learned a lot from her. Although our paths eventually parted, her response made my ad a smashing success.

Like my personal ad, my dates also revolved around food, My favorite activity was cooking dinner. I LOVED doing this, and especially at my place. No, it's not what you think; it wasn't a plot to be alone with a woman in a private spot. The presence of a woman in my apartment made it feel more like home, and that was what I was seeking.

Some women had the nerve to compare my food with that of former lovers. Linda said I was "almost" as good a chef as her second husband. Mary claimed her previous partner had a sharper eye for produce. And Susan spent an entire evening extolling a former lover's roasted asparagus.

More typically, however, dates praised my efforts. Some of them hadn't been cooked for by a man in years. They truly welcomed it. Sometimes, in fact, my cooking caused relationship problems because my thoughtfulness was misinterpreted. Once a friend had a particularly bad day. I decided to cheer her up by dropping off some chicken soup. To me, it was just a sweet gesture. To her, it was the equivalent of a marriage proposal.

Cooking frequently lays bare personality characteristics that might have otherwise remained hidden. For example, a Thanksgiving dinner exposed one woman's deceptive side. My hostess hated to cook, and bought the meal at the local grocer. It tasted fine, and I had a great time. She invited me again the following year, but said that she was making everything from scratch. Yet the food tasted eerily similar to that of the previous year. When I took out the garbage, I discovered the empty cartons from the supermarket.

Another woman could never delegate, and would actually verify my "spice loading" before allowing me to empty the contents of my spoon into the soup pot. And she had a thing about yeast, worrying incessantly if it was alive. This contrasted sharply with my more relaxed style, which was to generally take my yeast's health for granted.

Another woman was hypocritical on the issue of hygiene. She would get very upset with me if I used a tasting spoon to stir a pot. But this same lady sucks clean the nozzle from the Ready Whip container!

One relationship actually broke up due to philosophical differences about nutrition. I was dating a wonderful woman I nicknamed "Coronary Connie." I guess I should have been suspicious from the start, when I noticed that she served her gravy from a yacht. Or at least wised up when she attempted to pass off the Fudgsicle sticks lying all over her house as emery boards.

Connie never met a fat she didn't like. Donuts, cakes, and cookies were omnipresent. Two desserts per meal was the norm. And she didn't really GET it. One time when she was making grilled cheese sandwiches, I reminded her of the high levels of saturated fat in cheese. "Don't worry," she replied. "It's MILD cheddar."

UNSAFE ON ANY BURNER

When Connie and I eventually split, we needed to return each other's pots and pans. But Connie didn't cooperate. She always claimed to be too busy to schedule an appointment. Being no fool, I held onto her two candle holders, to assure her eventual cooperation.

After two months of delicate on-again, off-again negotiations, we finally met over coffee. As she joined me at the table, she clutched my pot tightly to her body. I, of course, brought the candle holders, but kept a fine eye on them, also. After the appropriate small talk, each of us slowly extended our right hands to give back our treasures, all the time synchronizing our pace to ensure we weren't giving up more than we were getting. I felt as if we were part of a Cold War spy exchange.

My left hand finally seized my precious pot. My fingers gently caressed it. I welcomed it home with a gentle kiss. Mission accomplished.

I raised my cup of decaf high, drew in a deep, reflectful breath, and smiled. At long last, I was a free man!

FREDDY'S TOP EIGHT DATING POINTS

- Never go out with a woman whose potholders are stain-free.

- Consomme is what couples do after guests leave.

- Obtain your lover's recipes PRIOR to the breakup.

- A man knows he's middle aged when the centerfold of Gourmet is of greater interest than that of Playboy.

- Excess use of a napkin is a crumby idea.

- Nothing breaks down barriers faster than a big bowl of chili.

- Real men don't cut sandwiches in half.

- The stove isn't all that gets turned on by co-ed cooking.

Waisted
Effort

It's All in the Jeans

An astonishing thing happened to me over the past four years in addition to discovering that I loved to cook. I lost fifty pounds (the easy part), and have actually kept it off (the hard part).

This was truly unprecedented. I'd been meaningfully overweight for most of the past thirty years, packing approximately two hundred and fifty-five pounds on my six-one frame. If someone had said I'd look trim in my lifetime, I'd have called him a liar.

How poor an eater was I? One of my sons nicknamed me HGP. It stands for "Human Garbage Pail." I merited the moniker because I routinely finished the leftovers on everyone's dinner plate.

Two stories might convince you I never met a

food group I didn't like. The first is from my travels in Europe. I was in a beautiful, four-star restaurant in the south of France. A gorgeous place. A reservation was difficult to procure. But there was a last-minute cancellation, so a visit was possible.

I dressed elegantly for the occasion, looking forward to enjoying the refined pleasures of French cuisine. Our reservation was honored promptly, and I anticipated the meal of a lifetime. However, as I waddled to the table, I sensed the raised eyebrows of many of the slender French diners.

The soup of the day was lobster bisque, my all-time favorite. Our tuxedoed server, Jacques, wheeled over a table holding a giant tureen filled with it. When he asked if I'd like a bowl, I responded with an overly enthusiastic "yes" that could be heard in the remotest corner of the establishment. Again the eyebrows.

I loved the soup. It was the best lobster bisque I'd ever tasted. I even felt happy for the lobster. I finished my bowl quickly.

A minute later, Jacques returned and offered a perfunctory, "Would you like more?" Apparently few diners are gauche enough to double dip. But I loved the soup. "Sure," I said. As Jacques took my empty bowl to the tureen, I sensed the collective, incredulous stares of my fellow diners. Jacques filled my bowl, but with far less flair than previously.

The second bowl was even more satisfying. "Gosh, what extraordinary soup," I said to myself. "Maybe I should try for thirds." Five minutes later the well-trained server returned and asked if I'd like another bowl. "Oui," I said, flashing my French.

Jacques looked surprised, spaced out. I half suspected a budding Cezanne might capture the moment as "Server And Tureen." Was it my order or my pronunciation? I feared Jacques might faint, falling smack dab in the middle of some unlucky diner's beef bourguignonne.

Fortunately, he snapped out of it, and ladled up my thirds. As he presented the bowl to me, he said, "Enjoy!" But his eyes clearly communicated, "How can you have thirds, American pig?"

Pigging out domestically wasn't foreign to me, either. About eight years ago, Mike and I were at Sam's Club and we came across a large bag of Famous Amos cookies. I'm talking large, perhaps thirty big cookies' worth. Mike and I both are chocaholics, so we looked at each other with the same devilish thought: "Should we get it?"

Duh. . .talk about your basic no brainer. "The cookies are for home," I told Mike. But when we returned to the car, neither of us could resist. We each ate two on the spot, and by the time the engine roared, we were craving more. "How about three for the road?" Mike said. "Fine," I answered.

Thus began a frenzied pattern of paying homage to landmarks along the ride home by disbursing additional cookies. As we passed County Stadium, Mike asked, "How about two cookies in honor of the Milwaukee Brewers?"

Two miles later Mike said, "How about two more to honor the Boys Club Tutoring Center?" And so it went, calorie after calorie. The low point came when I distributed a final cookie in honor of sighting a Wisconsin license plate (we were driving in Milwaukee).

So, you see, I was a certifiable big eater. But I confronted a conundrum. I had to reconcile my size with my self-concept as an attractive person. I resorted to the standard line of defense of the size-challenged: denial.

I extolled the nutritional benefits of my high-calorie diet. "Oreos have fiber," I'd claim. "Beef has protein." "Beer has barley." I became quite adept at making anything appear nutritious.

I specialized in "BUT I DON'TS." "Yes, I eat two big bags of potato chips a day, BUT I DON'T drink sugared colas." "Yes, I eat thirty-ounce steaks, BUT I DON'T put sour cream in my baked potato." "Yes, I rarely exercise, BUT I DON'T do drugs."

Basically, I fit the mold of the classic failed dieter.

UNSAFE ON ANY BURNER

I ate to excess. And couldn't keep off the pounds I would occasionally lose. And I possessed a litany of excuses to rationalize my appearance. In short, I was among the least likely to become a poster boy for healthy living.

But transform I did. It occurred during a conversation with Jessica. I was telling her about the death of a seventy-year-old acquaintance. I expressed a viewpoint that was needlessly harsh. "Of course, Bill's death is a tragedy," I said. "But I guess I'm not as sympathetic as I should be. He was a heavy smoker."

Jessica took umbrage at the comment. She thought it was a heartless thing for me to say. So she asked a simple question, the question that would turn my life around. "Why is his smoking any different than your weight?"

At first I was irritated. "Jessica," I said. "Everyone knows smoking causes lots of diseases. Bill could have stopped smoking at any time. If he had, he'd still be here for his wife, and kids, and grandkids."

"I agree," Jessica said, "but doesn't extra weight cause heart attacks, strokes, and diabetes? Isn't your lifestyle probably cutting short your potential time with Bob and Mike?"

I was about to give Jessica my response, when I realized I didn't have one. She was absolutely correct. Continuing to stuff my face was every bit as self-destructive as Bill's decision to smoke. Both bad habits carried known, substantial health risks. Only our poisons differed. Mine was food; his was nicotine.

Thus I was motivated to change my eating habits. The goal wasn't to lose a certain number of pounds. It wasn't to look good for a special occasion. It wasn't to lose weight for someone else. It was to live. Now when I looked at a big steak, I saw a heart attack robbing me of years with my children and future grandchildren. When I looked at sausage and cheese, I saw a potential stroke robbing me of my mind. When I looked at butter and mayonnaise, I saw diabetes and prostate cancer drastically limiting the quality of my senior years.

So I started eating healthy. This diet was so much different than any of my previous ones. I didn't have a goal for weight loss. There was no magic number at which I would declare myself handsome. This was not a diet about looks, it was a diet about life. And I would hopefully practice it forever.

Unlike prior diets, I ate normal food (details in next chapter). I didn't eat fifty-two grapefruit a day. Didn't eat liquid meals. Didn't buy portion controlled frozen dinners. Didn't weigh my food. Didn't compulsively count calories. Didn't take special food to parties. Didn't avoid restaurants. Didn't chew each bite six hundred times. Didn't starve myself. Didn't give up any favorite foods. Didn't weigh myself compulsively.

The only thing that concerned me was developing—at last—good eating habits. Otherwise, what was the point? The weight would just come back, as it always had before.

Thus started four years of essentially non-stop weight loss. I'm down about fifty pounds, and weigh 208. On my six-one frame, it works fine. Actually, I've probably lost more weight, but because I lift weights, it doesn't show on the scale (muscle weighs more than fat).

I can't tell you how wonderful it feels to be in control of my eating habits. That's a power I'd abrogated thirty years ago. I hope to never relinquish it again.

But be careful what you wish for! My transformation has produced immense satisfaction, but it has also created embarrassment. The satisfaction relates to my fantasy since college to wear a pair of regular-fit Levi's jeans.

As I began to lose weight, this dream surfaced again. Twice I prematurely tried on regular-fit jeans, with humiliating results. Each time I couldn't come close to fastening them. But as I kept losing weight, my dream still lived.

One magical day I was walking with Linda in the mall, and we passed a Levi's store. "Go try on a pair," she advised, aware of my fantasy. "Maybe they'll fit." I hesitated. It may sound ridiculous, but I was scared. What if my bubble burst again?

I approached a sales clerk, and asked where the regular-fit jeans were. There was no laughter, a good sign. I found a pair in light blue, my favorite color, and nervously approached the fitting room.

This time, size was with me. The pants fit! I'd done it. Linda was so happy for me she even paid for the jeans. I wore the miracle pants home from the store, and have practically lived in them since.

But now for the embarrassment. One day I saw a wonderful Speedo swimming suit at the mall, and I bought it. No, it's not what you think. It's not low cut, or whatever the term for a man would be. It's just a normal suit, but I loved the colors. And frankly, I thought I looked hot in it. Very hot.

I was at the Jewish Center lifting weights. My workout was especially fulfilling, as I'd increased the weight on two of my machines and encountered no difficulty. My custom is to take a whirlpool afterwards, and this day I was looking forward to parading out to the pool area in my new suit.

I strode with confidence to the showers, and permitted the warm water to comfort my chiselled body. I fantasized about my imminent, eye-pop-

175

UNSAFE ON ANY BURNER

ping entrance to the pool area. Brimming with confidence, I headed towards the whirlpool.

The response was electric, more than I thought
possible. Every female head turned. Was it my
imagination, or were the men jealously checking
me out also? I walked very slowly, to milk the attention.

Suddenly I saw the lifeguard approaching, seemingly intent on engaging me in conversation. "My
goodness," I said to myself. "Even she is going to
compliment me on my suit, and she sees suits all
the time!"

The lifeguard continued to approach, and
stopped close to me. She leaned towards me, and
in a confidential, concerned tone asked, "Are you
aware that you're naked?"

She was correct. In my excitement I left my hot
new suit hanging over a peg in the shower area.
No wonder people were looking. I rushed back to
put it on. I then meekly walked to the whirlpool,
allowing its warm waters to redden me further.

I learned a lesson that day. Weight loss is indeed
great, but never get so wrapped up in yourself that
you forget to wrap up.

FREDDY'S TOP EIGHT DIET POINTS

- Happiness is a big and tall store without mirrors.

- When the Devil tempted Eve, it's surprising he didn't use chocolate chip cookies.

- The only person you can lose weight for is yourself.

- Diet plans that promise quick, easy, and permanent weight loss prove Barnum correct.

- Eating low fat is a compromise you can live with.

- Never underestimate the number of stomachs an expensive blazer can hide.

- Losing weight is easy; keeping it off is the skill.

- Always check whether you're wearing your swimsuit before entering a coed pool.

The End of the Yo-Yo

I was as astonished as anyone that I finally developed good eating and exercise habits. Traditionally, I selected all-you-can-eat buffets by the length of the table, and the nearest I came to aerobics was rolling down the car window at the Burger King drive-thru.

Trying to learn from previous diet failures, I made few radical changes. I prohibited no foods. I made only reasonable sacrifices. And I allowed myself occasional binges.

I insisted that all foods be available to me, because I vividly recalled my ice cream winter. Back when I was in college, I started a diet in September. For four months I was perfect. Didn't enjoy a single forbidden calorie. Each day on the way home from class I'd walk by an ice cream store. Oh how I wanted a cone. Many times I put my hands on the front door, ready to rush toward my icy fantasy. I'd jealously eye lucky customers as they exited, flaunting their frozen treasures. Every day the store became tougher to ignore.

After months of deprivation, I met my weight loss goal. And guess where I went the next day? To the ice cream store. "I'll just have a one scoop cone," I confidently told myself. I entered the store on approximately January seventh. I left March fourth.

That experience taught me a lesson: don't forbid treats. In fact, I did just the opposite. I planned them.

I love bacon and eggs and hash browns. Six times a year, when I visit my Uncle Charley, I order them at the diner next to his house. The fact that I know they are still a dietary option keeps me, I think, from craving them more frequently.

Likewise with Hershey kisses. There's a neighborhood drugstore that sells them individually. In the past, whenever I'd walk by, I'd get a dozen. But that's a lot of fat. So now I only get four. I eat them slowly, and savor every morsel. They are more of a treat than ever.

Actually, when it came to cutting fat and calories, most of my work was automatically done for me. I demonized certain products as unhealthy—

cookies, donuts, sausage, frozen treats, cheese, mayonnaise, cream cheese, and butter (except for cooking), and avoided them as much as possible. All these foods happen to be very high in calories as well as fat. So most of what was left to eat was healthy by comparison.

I didn't have to make many other difficult decisions, except for one important thing. I established a list of compromises I was willing to live with:

For example, I decided not to buy chicken breasts that had skin on them. For too long I had cut off the skin of the cooked chicken at the table, only to eat the delicious morsels as dessert. By only buying skinless chicken breasts, I saved myself thousands of calories annually.

Gas stations had always tempted me, too. I would often turn them into candy stores. The issue for me wasn't regular or premium, but plain or peanut. I decided to pay at the pump, to avoid the calorie-rich insides of the stations.

Coffee was another compromise. In college I always drank it black, but more recently had switched to capuccinos, lattes, and cafe mochas. I resolved to go back to black, except for the first of every month, when I'd enjoy the largest cafe mocha I could find, with tons of whipped cream, just the way I like it. This approach saved me fat, calories, and a fair number of Starbucks.

I also limited all-you-can-eat buffets. Normally I'd go to a local Chinese restaurant once a week. I'd be good for thirds, even on my off days. But I began to feel self-conscious: fellow diners kept asking me for recommendations. My new aim was to indulge once a month. And as other, healthier restaurants became a habit, I now only dine at the Chinese restaurant once or twice a year.

At home I swore off salad dressings because they are full of calories and fat. And the bottles have such wide openings, it's impossible to pour just a little. As a substitute, I discovered lemon juice. By also adding cilantro and pepper to my salad, I have the taste I need with none of the fat or calories. When I eat a fancy meal out, I do have salad dressing, to help ensure I stay with my regimen at home.

I eliminated bread from my dinner meal. Not only do bread calories add up, but with bread goes butter, a fat no-no. After four days, I didn't really miss it. When presented with a bread basket in a restaurant, I take a roll, but with the consent of my fellow diners ask the server to remove what remains.

At the office I needed to find something to compete with the Honor Snacks box, which I confronted daily. It's chock full of cookies and chips and candy. So I brought in a bag of carrots and a few apples, and keep them in the small fridge near the snack box. During weak moments, at least fifty per cent of the time nutrition is victorious.

There were other compromises, too. I changed my milk consumption, going from two percent to one per cent or skim. I ate less beef, and more chicken, turkey, and fish. I always substituted mustard for mayonnaise, and never ordered a sub with cheese. I ate my bagels plain, or with honey or jelly.

But nothing was written in stone. I'd learned from my previous diets the importance of flexibility. Whenever I made a change, I'd invoke the "Five Day Rule." Unless I truly detested the substitute food, I'd stay with it for five days. This way, I'd give my taste buds a reasonably fair chance to adjust. After five days, if they still protested, I'd return to my old habits.

But I questioned the rule's wisdom when I attempted to substitute fat-free salad dressings for regular ones. My experience on Monday, Day One, was most unpleasant. I absolutely hated the artificial taste. Tuesday produced similar outrage; I felt sorry for the lettuce. But like a warrior, I persisted.

On Wednesday I sensed a great taste improvement. But as I complimented myself for my persistence, I noticed that in error I'd poured on the normal stuff. Thursday led to more unhappiness; I had to hypnotize the cherry tomatoes to get them to the salad plate. On Friday I found my lettuce cowering behind the orange juice. "Get out here,"

I said. "If I have to do this, you do also." We gave the fat-free dressing one last chance, and then rejoiced. Never again.

But often the "Five Day Rule" saved the day. Without it, I don't think I would have switched from bagels drenched with cream cheese to plain. The first day I ate a naked one and was appalled. "No taste," I said to myself. Same for Day Two. But by the third day, I was getting used to the change. And by the fifth, I was very comfortable with it.

Today I keep very few fattening foods around the house. When I'm desperate, the most trouble I can get into is raiding the crouton box or eating bread cubes unused at Thanksgiving. It's not that I don't occasionally eat candy or chips or ice cream. It's just that I do it when I'm out. That way, it remains a one-time thing, and I confront no ongoing daily temptation.

Of course when my boys are home for the summer, I have to have treats available. But I work smart. My favorite tactic is to put them in the back of the most remote and inaccessible cabinet (the treats, not the boys). That way they are out of sight and out of mind.

I also limit my temptation by purchasing snacks "just in time." If the boys are arriving at noon, I will buy the dangerous stuff that morning, and send any leftovers home with them.

But even with all these constructive changes, my diet would have been unsuccessful if I would have remained a couch potato. Fortunately, I joined a nearby health club. As I was aware that muscle burns more calories than fat, I wanted to lift weights, thereby building muscle and kicking my metabolism into overdrive. Three times a week I lifted. Soon, it became a habit; my car would automatically head for the club Mondays, Wednesdays, and Fridays.

In the weight room I avoided the free weights (they scared me), and just used the machines. As you may know, for each machine you can select the weight you desire. Wanting to establish a habit, I started very moderately. Slowly I added weight as my muscles became accustomed to the strain. I'd increase ten pounds (usually the minimum increment) every four months or so. That may not sound like much, but in a year, that's thirty pounds.

I've been lifting four years, and now lift a hundred and twenty more pounds on some machines than I did that first time. This weak little kid has actually maxed out three of the machines. It's incredible what habit can accomplish.

But building muscle wasn't the biggest advantage of my health club membership. It was forcing me to confront the locker room scale three times a week as I changed into my gym clothes.

You see, I have definite opinions on the use of a scale when dieting. In the past, I always weighed myself too often, two or three times a day. Inevitably, it would be a weigh-in that would doom my diet. I'd have been particularly "good" the prior day, yet the scale indicated weight gain. I'd conclude, "What's the use?" and head out for fast food. I would be forty pounds heavier by the time I next braved a scale.

This was now impossible. I gave away my scale at home, and thus couldn't weigh myself compulsively. But by regularly recording my weight three times a week as I changed into my gym clothes, I could be aware of any bingeing. Five times during the last four years I gained as much as eight pounds from a previous low. Each time I had to stand on that scale, record the new, greater weight, and resolve, "I haven't come this far to be fat again." And each time that resolve has returned me to the proper path.

In addition to lifting weights, I also moved more. Even on pleasant days, I walked up a storm. Weather permitting, I'd walk the half mile to my sub shop for lunch rather than driving. Paula loved to walk, and we frequently met at the local shopping mall. As long as we didn't venture within fifty feet of the food court, we were fine. And I asked a neighbor if I could occasionally walk his dog. Champ and I got along fine, and we each benefitted from the exercise.

But I built in daily walking in two specific ways that really became nice habits. When I'd stop for bagels in the morning, I'd park about a hundred yards from the store. And I'd do the same thing at work, parking in a distant part of the large lot.

A hundred yards may not sound like much, but remember, I'd walk it twice. Once getting to the bagel shop or office, and once returning to the car. So every day, I built in four hundred extra yards of exercise. That's over a mile a week, fifty miles a year! This was terrific for my health and my weight. Because it was done in small increments, I never even noticed I was doing it.

One day I was walking with Paula at the mall and we saw some treadmills. A light bulb went off. Why hadn't I thought of that? Years previous I had owned an exercise bike, and never used it. So I thought long and hard before making the purchase. But at this point I had two years of weight lifting and successful dieting behind me, and felt I now possessed the motivation and discipline to use the darn thing.

And use it I did! I love it. I walk forty-five minutes at a time, three times a week. Last year my goal was a hundred twenty sessions. This year, it's a hundred fifty. To keep me on track, I have a scratchpad near the treadmill. I keep a running total of my walks to date, and know that if I didn't, my goal would never be met.

I can't tell you how important the weight lifting and exercise have been to me. Without them, I would not have continued to eat healthy. I would be back at two hundred and fifty pounds, I guarantee it. So if you are planning a diet, please incorporate reasonable, doctor-approved exercise of your liking.

As you've doubtlessly sensed from the discussion above, I still don't have perfect discipline. Put a bag of potato chips in my house, and I'll demolish it that evening. And sometimes I skip a work out. But I think dieters are often too hard on themselves, and neglect to give themselves credit for the positive changes they make.

A recent experience at a Wendy's convinces me I'm on the right path. I stopped in for a small Frostee. The price was ninety-seven cents, and I placed my dollar on the counter. As the cashier was giving me my change, the manager approached. "You know," he said, "the medium Frostee is only two cents more. You're free to switch your order if you'd like."

The small price differential shocked me. I thought it was ridiculous. "I'm surprised there's so little difference," I said. But wanting to avoid the extra calories and fat, I indicated the small Frostee was fine.

But the well-meaning manager persisted. "You must not understand," he said. "The medium is almost fifty per cent larger. I'll even take two pennies out of the 'Take-A-Penny' jar for you."

My goodness, at this point I was being offered a free upgrade. That got me thinking. The larger size was the far better value. And I really love value. But I refused to bite.

With great pride and satisfaction I told him I preferred the small Frostee. It was what I came for. It was what I loved. It was what I wanted. And it was what I ate.

FREDDY'S TOP EIGHT NUTRITION POINTS

- A caramel apple a day doesn't keep the doctor away.

- It's best to start exercising before the stroke.

- Never pass up an opportunity to lay off calories onto co-workers.

- Just because you're slender doesn't mean your lifestyle is healthy.

- The other guy's metabolism is always faster.

- Buns of Steel are preferable to Rolls of Fat.

- The healthiest form of mayonnaise is mustard.

- Life is full of opportunities to order a small Frostee.

Final
Exam

Guess Who's Coming
to Dinner?

I don't remember when I first considered inviting the foremost restaurant critic in Wisconsin for dinner. I'm fairly certain alcohol was involved. I think I was having a pitcher of beer with Linda, and I asked a dangerous "what if" question.

"Linda," I said, "what if I invited Dennis Getto to dinner?" "Who?" she asked. "Dennis Getto," I repeated. "You know, the restaurant critic for the Milwaukee Journal Sentinel. Wouldn't that be a kick?"

Linda's laughter was immediate and loud, an excusable response, since she'd tasted my cooking. After composing herself, she said "I think it's a great idea." This was a pleasant surprise to me. Linda was fairly inflexible, and I thought she'd have trouble sympathizing with such a novel concept. "And afterward," she continued, "you can teach Miss Manners how to behave, Pavarotti how to sing, and the Pope how to pray." "Okay, okay," I said. "What's your point?"

Despite Linda's skepticism, the concept of hosting a professional food critic intrigued me. What a chance to test my recently acquired culinary skills! I called the Journal Sentinel, but Dennis was out. I left a message on his voice mail. "This may sound ridiculous, but I'm writing a humorous book about cooking, and would love to have you come to dinner and write a review of it." I left my name and number, and assumed I'd never hear from him.

I immediately regretted my call. "What am I getting myself into?" I asked. "I barely know a saucepan from a banana tree. I'll get the worst review in history. I hope he never calls."

My mind flashed back to the only other time I had dined with a celebrity. I was eating with the president of a local college, alone, in the gorgeous private dining room on campus. But this was no ordinary college; this was a Catholic college. And this was no ordinary president; this was a nun!

I was so nervous! Many Catholics would be intimidated, and I am Jewish. It was as if I was breaking bread with God. What should I say? How should I act?

Unfortunately, I set ecumenical relations back fifteen years. You see, I got in trouble with a fruit cup. The tuxedoed waiter placed a delicious-looking one in front of me, and I was veritably transfixed by the watermelon. It looked so incredibly tasty and delicious. I hurriedly reached for my spoon, and scooped up a piece. I raised the spoon to my lips, anticipating a burst of extraordinary sweetness as I bit into the fruit.

But as I took my first taste, two surprises occurred, one minor, one major. First, the minor one: the watermelon wasn't quite as delicious as I hoped. It really wasn't very sweet. This I could live with. But now the major one: as I was in mid-bite, my lunchmate, my hostess, the college president, the nun, began to say grace!

What to do? Pretend I hadn't started eating? Keep chewing? She must have seen me take my spoon to my mouth. Who wants to lie to a nun? I apologized profusely, and learned an important lesson that has stayed with me: never start eating before your hostess!

As I relived the embarrassment of this humiliating experience, the phone rang. It was Dennis. "I'd love to come to dinner," he said. "Sounds like fun. Most of my friends don't have the courage to invite me." What had I done?!

I asked Dennis about his background. I learned

he had been a restaurant critic for fifteen years (15!), and reviewed approximately two hundred restaurants annually. He'd studied with Simone Beck in Grasse, France, and had taken classes with Julia Child, Jacques Pepin, and Richard Grausman, the American representative of the famed Parisian cooking school, Le Cordon Bleu. He was familiar with all seven of Giuliano Bugialli's books on Italian cuisine, and he travelled frequently to Chicago for classes in Chinese and Thai cooking.

I immediately attempted to lower his expectations. "Dennis, I'm just a beginner," I confessed. "No problem," he reassured. "I always love new approaches." Approaches? What were they?

And then he asked me a few questions about my cooking background. "Fred, what's your favorite kind of cooking?" I now realize he was expecting answers like, "Middle Eastern," or "Northern Italian." I doubt he was impressed with my sincere but pathetic, "tasty."

He sighed, and asked if I regularly attended any local cooking demonstrations. My confidence rose. The previous week I observed an acclaimed local chef prepare a salmon dish with a lemongrass nage. I remember he identified a nage as a "court bouillon."

So I went with it. "Dennis, I haven't mastered court bouillon, or anything like that." "Oh yes," he

UNSAFE ON ANY BURNER

said. "Court bouillons. Short bouillons. These are quicker to prepare, shortened forms of traditional, classic bouillons." Dennis went on to say that "court" was the French word for short. News to me. I assumed a "court" bouillon was so named because it was enjoyed in the courts of Louis XIV!

I felt I should diminish his expectations for my homemaking, as well as my cooking. "Dennis, my apartment would not qualify for the cover of *Good Housekeeping*." But he wasn't scared off. "No problem," he said. "I'll keep my eyes focused on my dinner plate." I hoped he was true to his word, and made a mental note to have clean plates.

We quickly agreed on the ground rules. No money was to exchange hands. He could be brutally honest. And the review was just for my book, not for his paper.

Now that I had a guest, I needed a menu. I excitedly called my friends to ask for recipes and to brag about my guest. "Dennis Getto is coming; Dennis Getto is coming." I must have sounded like Paul Revere's cook!

My friends weren't as helpful with menu suggestions as I had hoped. Jessica lobbied for her "Risotto Medley," but I'd tried it and wouldn't serve it to Dennis' dog. Barb recommended her black bean soup, thinking that gas might detract attention from the taste. Mary suggested a good caterer.

I decided to cook only things I was very comfortable with. There would be enough pressure on me without attempting anything new. I chose to start off with the beautiful Spam Croustade, and follow up with my wonderful cauliflower soup with delicious won ton crackers.

I then would move into a salad course, with three kinds of lettuce, and Paula's Great Dressing. Next would come Thai Curried Chicken with Coconut Milk and Avocados, over rice. For dessert I'd offer two choices: lemon sorbet, in hollowed-out lemons, and Doris' Incredible Chocolate Fruit Tarts.

This menu may seem a tad eclectic, but I wanted to show Dennis my best. If I had merely cooked a Thai meal, for example, everything would have had to be Thai. By the way, if you'd like to make any of these dishes yourself, the recipes all appear earlier. Consult the Recipe Index in the rear of this book for the exact location.

One benefit of this menu was that many of the dishes could be prepared ahead of time: the soup, the salad, and the desserts. And the chicken entree needed little babysitting. This was important, as it would give additional time to spend with Dennis, Linda, and Gail and Ronnie, my friends from Chicago I'd invited to join us.

I asked Gail and Ronnie for strategy in confronting such a noted, knowledgeable diner. "Get him drunk!" Gail suggested. "Or burn his tongue on a very hot appetizer. He can't condemn what he can't taste." Ronnie took the phone. "Fred, don't worry," he said. "Regardless how something tastes, I'll say it's delicious." This strategy initially pleased me, but then I discarded it, fearing Dennis might think I'd planted shills. Ronnie's second suggestion was more realistic. "How about preparing exotic dishes he might never have tried? He'll have no basis for comparison, and assume they're supposed to taste that way!"

I thanked him for the thought, but informed him that my menu was set. However, I did follow through on one of Ronnie's suggestions: he had stressed the importance of a pretty table. I agreed. Anything to take Dennis' mind off the food.

Coincidentally, the Saturday before my brainstorm, I had bought eight new place mats. These consisted of checkerboard pastel squares in five colors: blue, red, orange, yellow, and green. Unfortunately, none of my cloth napkins complemented them well. Linda suggested that if I did go napkin hunting, I take the place mat along. "Do what?" I asked. "Take the place mat. It will help you find the right napkins." I was frightened by the concept. "Do guys do this?" I asked. "Don't turn macho on me," she said. "Do you want a great looking table or not?"

So, like a blushing bride, I headed off to Pier 1 with place mat in hand. I prayed I would run into nobody I knew. I purchased five different sets of napkins, and allowed Linda to make the decision as to which were best. She couldn't decide between the royal blue and the bright orange, so I kept both, and alternated them around the table.

In addition to cloth napkins, I wanted the flowers and candles to be perfect. I bought a lovely bouquet, and it beautifully graced the table center. I travelled to five stores before I found the proper shades of orange and blue candles to match the napkins.

But an attractive table by itself was insufficient; I needed also to present Dennis with surroundings that didn't inhibit his appetite. I actually dusted and vacuumed the public areas (even the places behind places), and felt rather proud of my efforts; the old apartment didn't look bad. And of course I touched up the bathroom—the mirror over the sink, the new soap tray. I discarded the house-brand tissue, and put out a fresh roll of Charmin.

I was so nervous the day before the event. What if Dennis laughed at my entree, or stormed out in disgust? I even had a nightmare. The disparate spices and flavorings I have formed into a marinade turn toxic. As Dennis takes his first bite, he falls over, clutching his throat. "What have you done to me?" he gasps. Ron and I subsequently carry him five miles to a hospital in the midst of a giant thunderstorm (apparently I don't drive when I dream). Dennis' stomach gets pumped, and he, thankfully, survives. I pray no one will find out about the incident, but as I wake up, Dennis is laying out a special edition of his newspaper with the whole story!

Despite all my worry and preparation, it was the food that would make or break the evening. I really went overboard on the salad, buying orange, red, and yellow bell peppers. I purchased three different kinds of lettuce: bibb, Boston, and red leaf. What with the cherry tomatoes, seedless cucumbers ($1.89 each!), mushrooms, and grated carrot, the salad was going to be gorgeous.

The chocolate fruit tarts also received more than usual attention. Even though I was only preparing five, and these are small, I bought honeydew, cantaloupe, watermelon, raspberries, blueberries, blackberries, and strawberries. Because it was November in Wisconsin, I don't even want to think what each tart cost. I painstakingly decorated each tartlet, arranging each piece of fruit so it was surrounded by the other varieties.

I even fretted over the beverages. Uncharacteristically, I bought an expensive bottle of merlot. It turned out to be delicious. I cleaned the coffee pot thoroughly, in case Dennis liked java with dessert. And I even put a fresh filter in my Brita pitcher, hoping that the tasty, clear water would freshen his palate to my advantage.

Unfortunately, I left all the slicing and dicing to just four hours before the dinner, and it took longer than I anticipated. Partly this was due to an amazing coincidence. For three weeks I'd been "nursing" a bottle of dishwashing liquid. I kept forgetting to buy a new container, and I meted out the precious remaining drops as needed.

With all my preparation, my sink became cluttered with dirty dishes. I needed to wash them, both to clear the sink, and because I needed to reuse some of the dishes. But when I went to put dishwashing liquid on my sponge, I was "Dropless in Getto Land." I squeezed and squeezed, but nothing emerged. Perhaps the bottle was intimidated by Dennis, too. Of all the days to run out of dishwashing liquid! So I had to rush to the store, losing twenty-five precious minutes in the process.

My friends kept calling, too, wishing me well but pushing me further behind schedule. Linda tried to prepare me for the nuances of food critic speak. "Now don't be upset if he says something is 'interesting,'" she said. "That's good." "What do you mean?" I asked. "I say my Aunt Mary's hair looks 'interesting,' when she really looks horrible." But Linda was insistent. "And remember, 'not bad' means 'good.'" I was on to Linda's plan. Take disappointment out of play by defining any comment Dennis might make as favorable.

As a result of all these interruptions, five minutes before Dennis' arrival time, I was still setting the table. Unbeknownst to me, he was outside, watching me race frantically about. He later wrote in the review he sent me:

> As I stood in the courtyard, a shadowy figure dashed past the window above me clutching a handful of silverware. The tightly clenched knives and forks looked like a metallic bouquet.

Dennis rang the buzzer, and I welcomed him. I took his coat, and introduced him to Linda, Gail, and Ron. Unfortunately, the evening got off to an embarrassing start. You see, I was running so late, I was forced to take a very rushed shower, and neglected to dry myself thoroughly.

Linda immediately remarked that moisture showed through the back of my turtleneck, but I assumed it would dry quickly, and that she was exaggerating its prominence. But apparently I really looked strange. Dennis took one look at me and asked, "Did you have an explosion in the kitchen? You're all wet in back." I fessed up to him about my poor planning, and we all had a good laugh. The evening could only go uphill!

We then sat down in the living room to eat the Croustade, hot from the oven. I kept Dennis in suspense about the secret ingredient, Spam. Here's what he wrote:

> Gosman appeared with a beautifully browned phyllo pastry. I rolled the cheese over my tongue and detected the first small piece of meat. "What is this?" I asked, half fearing the answer. "Spam," Gosman responded. I panicked. How much did I know about this Gosman fellow? Was he a Spam freak? Would this dinner be a rewrite of the famous Monty Python sketch about a restaurant that only serves odd dishes made with Spam?

Unfortunately, Dennis was not a Spam lover. He'd hated it since age six. Gail and Ronnie, however, both took seconds (bless them), and I took thirds. But I'm not sure it counted for much if we liked it!

After twenty minutes of pleasant conversation, we moved to the table, for the thankfully Spam-free cauliflower soup, with wonderful won ton crackers. Dennis thought the soup "not bad," and the won ton crackers "pleasantly crunchy." In his review, he said the soup would have benefitted from some fat.

I think he has a point. I'm used to cooking low fat, and the spicy soup, with its cumin, curry, and pepper, is quite tasty to me. But a little cream or butter, added into the large soup pot and divided between six servings, would probably produce a more pleasing taste to those not requiring strict fat restriction.

Fortunately, the salad met with his favor, as did the dressing:

The salad was very interesting, with strips of yellow, orange, and red pepper. And the vinaigrette was tasty.

Thank goodness I had popped for the bell peppers, and used Paula's great dressing!

As Gail and Ronnie engaged Dennis in conversation, Linda and I went into the kitchen to check on the Thai chicken dish. Disaster awaited us!

I was anxious to get back to Dennis. In my hurry, when I added the cut-up chicken to the wok, I did it from eight inches above. When it all plopped into the wok at once, coconut milk came pouring over the sides. With uncanny accuracy, it sought out the most inconvenient resting place, Linda's boots. She was a sport (with spotty boots), and recognized my chicken-dumping error as that of a nervous cook. But as we brought the entree to the table, we both hoped Dennis wasn't a leg man.

The chicken dish produced another "not bad" ("probably good?") from Dennis, although Gail and Ronnie and Linda and I all had seconds (as I think Dennis did!). As he wrote:

> *Gosman made several common gaffes. Jasmine rice is the rice of preference with Thai food. And Thais never eat with chopsticks. The dish would have benefitted from Thai fish sauce. Thai curry without fish sauce is like an American hamburger without the bun. And flavor was lost because of the substitution of low fat coconut milk.*

Other than that, he loved it! Dennis, thanks for letting me know about the jasmine rice and chopsticks. I was unaware. The recipe, surprisingly, doesn't call for fish sauce, but I'm willing to add a little (very little, because it stinks!) the next time I make it. I'll continue to avoid full-bodied coconut milk, however. It's just loaded with fat.

A very unique aspect of the meal was trying to spy on Dennis unobtrusively, to determine what he really liked. I'd pretend to be speaking to Gail on my right, but all the time out of the corner of my left eye I'd furtively note the rate of Dennis' utensil movements. But I lacked enough information to make helpful interpretations. How fast did he eat normally? And was a long pause after a first forkfull a sign of displeasure, or was he merely allowing time for his sophisticated palate to make a knowledgeable diagnosis?

The desserts certainly pleased Dennis, so we finished with a winner:

The dinner ended on a bright note. Gosman served a light, excellent lemon ice, and small, fruit-topped tartlets. In the filling beneath the fruit I was sure I was tasting real fat for the first time in five courses.

Great, Dennis, the only "excellent" you give me is for the lemon ice, the one item that was store bought. No wonder your friends don't have you for dinner!

Seriously, I was pleased that he liked the desserts. The lemon ice is a no brainer, and it's fun to serve in hollowed-out lemons. The tartlets are a little more work, but everyone always loves them.

Dennis gave the meal two overall grades, one for taste, one for ambiance. Both pleased me. He said the meal was "better than many I've had in middle-of-the-road restaurants." I can live with that.

But it was his other grade that interested me more, the one for ambiance:

FRED GOSMAN

While the food wasn't four star, the company was. Fred did everything to make his guests comfortable in a very unique situation. Everyone was relaxed, and we all had a very pleasant evening.

Dennis, I thank you. For all of your comments. You were a great sport, dared to speak honestly, and gave me one of the more interesting evenings of my life. Although I know my cooking still has far to go, you provided me with a powerful reminder of exactly how far I've come.

FREDDY'S TOP EIGHT
IMPORTANT DINNER TIPS

- Interpret any review that doesn't include a skull and crossbones as "good."

- Always throw the host bouquets, even if there are flowers present.

- Never trust a skinny food critic.

- Always give the celebrity the least dirty place mat.

- A food critic who has thirds shouldn't complain about the taste.

- Mystery meat is not a good choice for an elegant dinner.

- Always slide chicken into a wok.

- Don't skimp on dessert—buy the best lemon ice you can.

Let's Share

So, what did you think of this book, and its recipes? I'd love to hear from you. And do you have any funny cooking experiences? I would adore hearing them.

How about recipes? Do you have a family treasure? Have you concocted a quirky, special wonder? If I like the recipe, perhaps I could include it in my next book.

Send comments and recipes to Fred Gosman at P.O. Box 11558, Milwaukee, WI 53211. Or e-mail me at:

FG@FredGosman.com

These addresses can also be used to contact me about presenting a humorous talk on cooking, food,

UNSAFE ON ANY BURNER

or nutrition to your group or association.

HERE'S THE DEAL! In return for your input, I'll share (if you're brave enough). On each of the first three anniversaries of the publication of this book, I'll select the name of someone who has sent me a letter or e-mail. I'll come to that person's home sometime in the following twelve months, to prepare full dinner for eight! I'll buy all the groceries, and do all the prep and clean up.

As with Dennis Getto, the restaurant critic, I can't promise a four-star meal. But I can deliver a four-star time! I look forward to saying "Bon Appetit."

Recipe Index